A PORTRAIT OF
DORIAN YATES

The Life and Training Philosophy of the World's Best Bodybuilder

By Six-Time Mr. Olympia
Dorian Yates
with Peter McGough

The Ultimate Bodybuilding Guide
from the Ultimate Bodybuilder

Copyright © 2006 Dorian Yates Limited

All rights reserved including the right of reproduction
in whole or in part in any form.

Dorian Yates Limited,
16 Temple Street
Birmingham B2 5BY
England

Text Layout and Design by
Alex McKenna (of Muscle News)
Photo Credits:
Kevin Horton, Chris Lund and Roger Shelley
Cover Photos:
Chris Lund (front), **Kevin Horton** (back).

A Portrait of
DORIAN YATES

The Ultimate Bodybuilding Guide from the Ultimate Bodybuilder

This instructional/motivational book is intended as a guide for building maximum muscle mass. The information it contains and the training principles it advocates are intense. In no way – either written or implied – should this book be used to replace the advice from a medical professional. Always consult your physician before beginning any exercise program.
Adjust all poundages and intensity accordingly. Beginning and intermediate bodybuilders should never attempt to duplicate a professional's training program.

Acknowledgments

From Dorian:

To Deb, Lewis and Mom for always being there and for giving a focus for my efforts; Joe and Ben Weider for creating the sport we all enjoy and for giving me the opportunities I have had; Wayne DeMilia of the IFBB and Jim Manion of the NPC for their counsel and support; Steve Weinberger and Bev Francis for their friendship and loyalty, and all at Gold's Gym, Syosset, New York; Chris Lund and Kevin Horton for their great photography; Peter McGough and all at FLEX, especially George DePirro, Jim Schmaltz, Dave Standel, and Cinnamon Howard who aided in the compilation of this book; Anne Byron for putting up with Peter McGough's seclusion during the writing of this book; Tom Deters and all at Muscle & Fitness; Kerry Kayes, Dave Parry and all at Chemical Warfare; Gary and Daisy Gideon for their friendship and enthusiasm; Naeem Qureshi at Olympian Distribution; Leroy and the gang at Temple gym; and not least all the fans for their invaluable encouragement.

Contents

Foreword ix

Introduction xi

SECTION ONE: THE MAN by Peter McGough

Chapter 1 THE AWAKENING ....Page 1

Chapter 2 THE GATHERING SHADOW ....Page 7

Chapter 3 FIVE SANDOWS AND A LEGEND ....Page 15

Chapter 4 THE ULTIMATE WARRIOR ....Page 25

SECTION TWO: THE MUSCLE by Dorian Yates

Chapter 5 RECUPERATION: Bodybuilding's Big Secret ....Page 33

Chapter 6 THE BUILDING BLOCKS: Training Principles ....Page 41

Chapter 7 THE FULL MONTY: My Complete Training Program ....Page 47

Chapter 8 STARTING OUT: Complete Training and Diet Program for Beginners ....Page 57

Chapter 9 THE ADVANCED LEVEL: Complete Training and Diet Program ....Page 67

Chapter 10 ON GIANT SHOULDERS: Deltoids and Traps ....Page 75

Chapter 11 TRI, TRI, AND TRI AGAIN: Triceps ....Page 83

Chapter 12 THE MIDDLE GROUND: Abdominals ....Page 89

Chapter 13 LOOK OUT, BEHIND YOU!: Back ....Page 93

Chapter 14 PEC POWER: Chest ....Page 101

Chapter 15 SMOKIN' GUNS: Biceps ....Page 107

Chapter 16 THE WORKOUT FROM HELL: Quads, Hamstrings and Calves ....Page 113

Chapter 17 NUTRITION FOR MASS ....Page 123

Chapter 18 MUSCLE INK: The Need To Keep A Diary ....Page 131

Chapter 19 DEVELOPING AN IRON WILL ....Page 137

Chapter 20 AT THE END OF THE DAY ....Page 143

Foreword

What Makes Dorian Run?

I was 11, and my school had organized a noontime sponsored run that coincided with the day of the 1973 FA Cup Soccer Final [England's equivalent of the Super Bowl]. The run involved laps around a 400-meter track. After 15 laps, I was the only runner left. I felt tired, but I thought, No, I gotta keep going, I gotta keep going. The soccer match was due to start at three o'clock. Before two o'clock, most of the onlookers had left to go home in time to see the match. Finally, the only ones left at the track were me and the teacher supervising the run. At 30 laps, he began shouting, "Come on! That's enough, I want to go home or I'll miss the match." I shouted back, "Just let me see how many laps I can do." I was hurting, but I was consumed with finding out how many laps I could dig in for, and how tough I was physically and mentally. Finally, after 45 laps (nearly 11 1/4 miles), the teacher forced me to quit the run so he could leave and watch the soccer final. I was disappointed because I knew I had a few more laps left in me. At 11 years of age, I had learned something of myself: I had an aptitude for an endeavor that combined physical and mental strength. Ten years later, I was to find the perfect arena in which to exercise that aptitude: Bodybuilding!

– Dorian Yates, Mr. Olympia (1992-97)

Introduction

With the current proliferation of bodybuilding and fitness books, what makes the words of Dorian Yates so meaningful? Well, for starters, with six Mr. Olympia victories, he has dominated bodybuilding in the '90s in the manner that Arnold Schwarzenegger (seven Olympia wins) dominated the '70s and Lee Haney (eight Olympia wins) dominated the '80s. Furthermore, he dominated his sport in a white-hot period of competition when the standards have never been higher. Notwithstanding his contest track record, Dorian's true legacy will be his training philosophy.

He brought a scientific and precise planning approach to bodybuilding that revolutionized the sport. He took as his base Mike Mentzer's Heavy Duty training creed and modified it to his own design and beliefs. Previous to Dorian, bodybuilding's most popular workout plan involved training six days a week, employing 20 or so sets per bodypart. He built the world's best-ever physique with short intense workouts that comprise only one all-out set for each exercise, and only two or three exercises per bodypart. He trains only once a day, four days a week. He overturned the more-is-better school of thought by proving that the most important component in the muscle-building process is the need for proper recuperation.

Dorian was also a pioneer in combining cardio work with bodybuilding. In turn, this led to him helping to develop the modern bodybuilding diet, wherein the contest-prep diet does not involve a drastic reduction in calories from the offseason diet. No longer do bodybuilders need to starve themselves in the last few weeks of a contest diet. In the gym and onstage, he's the supreme competitor, and it's likely that no bodybuilder ever trained harder or smarter, or exploited his genetic potential to a greater extent than Yates. Some may question the previous statement by pointing to his list of injuries, but that merely underlines his unyielding determination in exploring his limits. And who else would have the heart to overcome the injuries he's sustained? By doing so, Dorian proved he is the sport's ultimate warrior.

In addition to his training and diet innovations, Yates imbued the role of Mr. Olympia with both a nobility and a working-class hero's common touch. His physique and his articles in Joe Weider's FLEX and MUSCLE & FITNESS magazines have made him the most inspirational and popular bodybuilder on the planet, as well as the champion listened to the most. Dorian Yates bucked the trend, stayed true to his roots and beliefs, and did it his way, and only his way. By doing so, he made history by becoming the first Mr. Olympia to ever hold the title while living outside of the United States.

On a personal note: Perhaps his greatest accomplishment, in this age of sporting superstars and oversized egos, is that, despite his lofty achievements, the six-time Mr. Olympia remains today, at age 36, the same well-balanced, unpretentious and enthusiastic person whom I first met when he was 23 and at the start of his career. Dorian Yates is a man who is and who will continue to be a role model for and a credit to the sport of bodybuilding. This is a man in every sense of the word. This is a man worth listening to.

– Peter McGough, FLEX Editor in Chief

Dorian, aged 11, with sister Lisa and Shadow

CHAPTER 1

THE AWAKENING

"You're a damn liar, Yates!" barked the reform-school officer. "Nobody could do three circuits that quickly!" The circuit referred to was the series of weight-training exercises Dorian Yates and the other 20 inmates in his block had been ordered to do. While the future Mr. Olympia had completed three of the circuits with ease, none of his compatriots had finished one. Nineteen-year-old Dorian Yates knew it was futile to argue with cynical uniformed authority. It was time to shut up and put up.

Thus, he again, this time under the beady-eyed watch of the disbeliever, completed another two circuits with super-quick speed.

"Hmm," the reform-school officer grudgingly acknowledged, "you're a natural at this weight-training game, son!" The officer (for the benefit of this narrative, we'll call him Potter) knew what he was talking about, as he was the driving force behind the weight-training and powerlifting program at Whatton Youth Detention Centre, a reform school for juvenile offenders in the East Midlands region of England, in which Yates found himself incarcerated during the summer of 1981.

"A natural?" mused the youngster as he recalled the flirtation he had experienced with the world of barbells three years before. In 1978, he had by chance seen a black-and-white photo of Robby Robinson in a copy of *Muscle Builder/Power* (now *Muscle & Fitness*) and had been so inspired that he "dabbled with weights" for six months before moving on to karate.

He'd never forgotten the special buzz that gym work had given him and, after Potter's commendation, he had fresh reason to reflect on that episode in his life and the circumstances that surrounded it.

A PORTRAIT OF DORIAN YATES   **1**

GO AHEAD, PUNK, MAKE YOUR DAY

Dorian Yates was born on April 19, 1962, in the rural village of Hurley, near Tamworth, about 20 miles from Birmingham, Britain's second-largest city. His father was a commercial pilot. His mother ran her own horse- riding school, and Dorian's younger sister was to become an accomplished horsewoman of some repute. While the accepted Yates folklore is that he is a pug-made-good from the backstreets of Birmingham, the truth is Dorian Yates had an upbringing that was more Wuthering Heights than West Side Story. Even as he lived the rustic lifestyle for the first 16 years of his existence, Dorian knew that he was different.

In 1975, his father died after a long illness and, in 1978, Dorian moved with his mother and sister from Hurley to Birmingham, one of Britain's toughest and most-forbidding cities.

After only a few months of big-city life, Dorian's mother decided Birmingham was not for her, so she returned to her rural roots. Her 16-year-old son, with the stubborn streak of independence that newly burgeoning hormones bring, opted to stay in Birmingham. For this country boy, the roar and energy of a metropolis beat the hell out of the pastoral calm he had known in his formative years.

In Britain, the late '70s represented a time of sweeping political change. A beleaguered Labour government was embroiled in its death throes, making ready for the advent of radical Margaret Thatcher, and in that fermenting atmosphere of ringing out the old and bringing in the new, the nation's teenagers grasped at a new confrontational ideology. The punk-rock movement was born. The newly independent Dorian empathized with the doctrine – or, more correctly, lack of doctrine – of this new crusade and dutifully donned the appropriate uniform: shaved head, Doc Martens boots and obligatory tattoos.

The punk-rock atmosphere of the time had nothing to do with the neo-Nazi skinhead beliefs that such shaved-head and tattooed credentials now generally signify. Indeed, upon his mother's departure from Birmingham, Dorian moved into the family home of a black friend named Adrian. Punk rockers flexed no color prejudice. For them, the credibility gap was not one of race, it was one of generation.

Dorian found intermittent work at a succession of construction sites, the lack of permanence dictated by the punk code that declared that he be argumentative and defiant in the face of authority. For him and his merry crew, the guiding lights were the Sex Pistols in general and Sid Vicious in particular. Today, Dorian ruefully comments, "The first bodypart I ever developed to an extreme was the huge chip on my shoulder." He endured periods of unemployment and even a stint working at a slaughterhouse.

His nights centered around gang life. Several times a week, the 15 or so who represented his circle would invade Birmingham's city center, hit the pubs and drink – sometimes almost into oblivion. Alcohol's unpredictable influence often led to trouble. Yates remembers the time: "Guys got drunk, then got verbal, and before anyone knew what was happening, a fight would break out, either among individuals or with a rival gang."

Despite the activity, the harum-scarum reveler of the previous evening often would wake up on cold, cheerless mornings with the effects of the alcohol still clouding his consciousness and ponder, This life is not for me: I'm different.

DEAD AT 21

On February 2, 1979, Sex Pistols bassist Sid Vicious died from a drug overdose. With their antihero dead at 21, Dorian and his fellow insurrectionists took an even more fatalistic view of life. "With Sid

Vicious dying at that age, our attitude was that we didn't care if we lived after we were 21 either. There seemed to be nothing to offer after that. To look forward to settling down, having a family and a house seemed like BS. I got into a lot of scrapes and got away with a lot of things because I just didn't care. I was unconcerned with the repercussions of my actions. I had nothing to lose . . . life ended at 21."

After a year at Adrian's house, Dorian moved into a one-room bed-sit in a notorious area of Birmingham. The uninviting room – part of a dark and somber Victorian house that had known much better days – contained a single bed, a gas fire and a chair. Adrian helped Dorian move in, and upon viewing the dismal high-ceilinged room, he remarked to the new tenant, "Christ, Dorian! This is the kind of place someone moves into and hangs himself."

"Thanks, pal," responded Dorian. "That'll help me sleep a bit better."

With his new home so unappealing, Dorian found even more reason to search for diversionary activities. Pretty soon, he was in the clubs and pubs every night, drinking and partying at every opportunity: Live for today, life ends at 21.

Inebriation became a form of release, and drugs of the soft variety soon became another commodity that was not taboo to his group. Dorian himself never went overboard on the latter. His use was mainly in the spirit of being one of the boys, but unlike Bill Clinton, Dorian admits to inhaling. However, as is the classic pattern, some of his acquaintances went from soft to hard drug use. Today, a couple are heroin addicts, while others have disappeared from the face of the planet in some way or another.

Dorian tried to support himself by holding down a job as best as his rebellious nature would allow. But some of his contemporaries preferred unemployment and, looking for alternative sources of revenue, began drifting into the criminal underworld, committing burglaries and the like.

The fights and incidents became more common. Dorian was arrested for being drunk and disorderly, and as the new decade of the '80s dawned, he really did not give a damn if he lived to see the '90s.

Only in later years has the six-time Mr. Olympia been able to rationalize his reckless lifestyle of the time. Being out of his brains was an escape from the futility and loneliness he felt. The alternative was to dwell in his miserable bed-sit and stare at its four walls. Being a punk and part of a gang gave him a sense of identity, a sense of belonging that acted as a substitute for the family that had moved back to village life.

At the time, Dorian was so full of bravado that he would not admit to anyone else that he was unhappy, but in more quiet, ruminatory moments, he knew that he was. In tandem with that unhappiness was the realization that he was different, that life had something better in store for him and that somehow, in some way, he would rise above the rut of the existence he had fallen into.

LIFE'S A RIOT

Dorian Yates' watershed moment occurred during the fateful summer of 1981, when major riots, generated by social unrest and seemingly engineered by self-serving militant factions, broke out in the major cities of Britain. In scenes of unprecedented mayhem, squads of police fought mob violence in the street, countless properties were razed and looting was rife.

Against that background, Dorian and a friend found themselves in Birmingham's besieged city center at midnight, en route to a party. In a state of partial inebriation, they came across a smashed shop window (the result of a mini riot that had occurred earlier) from which a clothes dummy was hanging half out. The shop was Dunne's: a men's emporium that caters to Britain's affluent hunting, shooting and fishing set. For a giggle, the twosome decided to take the bowler hat and cravat worn by the mannequin and wear them to the party. It would make their pals laugh to see two revolutionary punks garbed in the apparel of the toffee-nosed upper classes.

As Dorian's compadre tried to divest the dummy of the required items, it toppled completely out of the window; what was left of the glass shattered with a mighty crash. Almost immediately, the bemused duo were surrounded by a score of riot police. There were no ifs, ands or buts: In the recriminatory mood of the times, Yates and his associate were sentenced to six months at Whatton Youth Detention Centre.

Of the affair, Dorian says: "It was a case of being in the wrong place at the wrong time. But whether I should have been sent down for that incident or not, my behavior over the previous couple of years probably merited some form of punishment."

Thus, with his life going nowhere, fate decreed that the young rebel who deep down knew that he was "different" be ensconced in an institution that prided itself on its tradition of powerlifting and weight-training success.

BARS & BARBELLS

With the early demonstration (vis-à-vis his prowess at circuit training detailed earlier) of his aptitude for the discipline of weight-training, Dorian earned an instant reputation as the strongest and fittest of Whatton's 300 inmates. This gave him a new respect for himself as well as earning him the respect of the prison staff, especially Potter, the head of the weight-training program, who had at first been so skeptical of the new detainee's efforts.

"It was like a switch had activated a voice in my head that said, 'Maybe weights are what makes you different.'" The former "dead at 21" advocate resolved that when he was released, he would sort out his life and end his lemminglike behavior. "Whatton was a wake-up call that made me realize that I was sliding down a slippery slope," he says. "If I didn't do something about it, I could end up the same way as some of the other inmates, who were destined to be in and out of prison all their lives."

Due to his exemplary conduct, Yates served only four months of the six-month sentence. On the day he walked out of the prison gates, Potter told him, "You don't belong in here with most of this lot, son. You're different."

Dorian knew he was different. He also knew he would not be back.

TOWARD BODYBUILDING

During his time in Whatton, the iron bug had sunk its teeth firmly into Yates. The virus would lie dormant, incubating for 18 months or so, until other practical aspects of his life were in order.

Upon his release in late '81, Dorian and a Rastafarian friend, Choc, moved into a new council flat housed in a large apartment block. By early 1982, Dorian was holding down a full-time job as an industrial cleaner, which he would stay with for more than two years.

"It was a physical job, involving a lot of lifting and very, very dirty," says Dorian. "After I was made redundant [laid off], it took about a year to get the dirt out of my skin."

For entertainment, he still went out regularly, but not every night and he stopped getting drunk. His drinking was strictly social. Nowadays, Yates may drink a glass of wine only three or four times a year. He let his hair grow and no longer felt the need to submerge his personality into the collective identity of a group. He was "different," an individual committed to doing things his way.

In January 1983, he met his future wife, Debbie Chinn, and the couple were to forge a bond that became unbreakable. Their union was blessed with the arrival of son Lewis in May 1984.

Four months after meeting Debbie, with his nightclubbing days a thing of the past, a job that gave him security and a relationship that gave him a future, Yates knew the direction of the path that would prove how he was "different." He decided to start bodybuilding. Serious bodybuilding!

His bodybuilding induction had been two years in the making and was not typical. Once he'd made the decision to bodybuild, he didn't enter a gym for nearly a month. Instead, he sought out and absorbed every available piece of literature he could find on the subject, an early indication that for "Dorian Yates: Bodybuilder," preparation and planning is everything.

From his first day of entering the gym with serious intentions, he was totally focused on realizing his destiny and becoming the best competitive bodybuilder he could be. He wanted to see how far being "different" could take him. It was to take him all the way.

CHAPTER 2

THE GATHERING SHADOW

In the summer of 1983, six months into their relationship, Dorian told Debbie he was going to start bodybuilding. He still can't fully explain the reasoning and timing for the impulse: "Most fundamental decisions have a natural order to them involving no soul-searching." To the news, Debbie nodded in acquiescence; from day one of their union, she's never stopped Dorian from doing what he wanted to do.

The entry of Dorian Yates into bodybuilding was far from typical. He didn't go near a weight for three weeks. Instead, his mission was to absorb every piece of information he could glean from the available literature. He didn't slip into the sport by degree. From the first day he took his 5'10", 180-pound frame into the gym, Dorian was focused 100% on being a bodybuilder. He was not there to supplement another sport. He was not there to keep fit; he was not there to train arms to look impressive in a T-shirt. None of the traditional bodybuilding inductions applied to Dorian Yates. He was there to be a bodybuilder, to be different.

Working out three times a week, his biggest influence was Mike Mentzer's Heavy Duty System, which called for intense workouts of short duration. Dorian made rapid progress and thought he might have the potential to compete someday, although his loftiest ambition at the time was that he might be good enough to enter the local Mr. Birmingham contest three or four years hence. A few weeks after commencing training, he was an enthralled spectator at the '83 British Championships, as then-current sensations Angelito Lesta – the winner – and Ian Dowe went down to the wire in pursuit of the light-heavyweight crown. The apprentice watched the flexing duo and concluded, "These guys are huge –

A PORTRAIT OF DORIAN YATES 7

out of touch for the likes of me!" and contented himself that his goal was simply to be the best his potential allowed.

Despite this low self-estimation and even lower profile, rumors began to emanate from Birmingham toward the end of 1984 that there was a young guy making gains that were unbelievable. Such stories are a regular part of the bodybuilding grapevine; the "experts" dismissed the glowing references.

A STAR IS BORN

Dorian Yates' explosion onto the competitive scene has been enshrined in British bodybuilding folklore. In July 1985, he entered the intermediate class of the West Coast Championships in Morecambe, Lancashire, and his 210-pound blend of mass, shape and quality caused a sensation. Observers were united in the opinion that the physique before them would be a shoo-in to take the British heavyweight title, never mind the day's intermediate class. Coming offstage, the novice was petitioned by officials to be part of the English team for the following weekend's World Games in London. A mental check of the calendar assured the first-timer it wasn't April 1, and he attempted to explain that all this attention was surely unnecessary. Nevertheless, he found himself propelled onto the English squad for the imminent World Games. (Journalists dream of being there the day a star is born. Dorian's day at Morecambe was also my day.)

Dorian didn't enjoy his participation in the World Games, but the experience was pivotal to his education. From day one of commencing bodybuilding, he had advocated meticulous planning down to the smallest detail. He hadn't planned for the World Games. His strategy for 1985 was to compete at the British Intermediate Finals, which he became ineligible for by being selected for the national team.

Even as Dorian pumped up backstage at the Wembley Conference Centre for the World Games, he felt the urge to tell everybody, "I shouldn't be here, you know. I've been training only two years; this is my second contest." In the World Games heavyweight division, those who would have been shocked by this information included Berry DeMey, Matt Mendenhall, Olev Annus and Selwyn Cottrell.

Taking stock of his situation, the novice promised himself, This will never happen again. His mentality dictated that he go into each specific contest as a winner, or not at all. Dorian didn't feel like a winner at the World Games. He knew his condition had faded in the week since Morecambe, and he had reluctantly agreed to compete only in response to experienced voices saying it would be a good career move. His eventual seventh-place finish didn't merit a trophy, but he came away from the World Games with an even more valuable prize: the iron resolve to never again be distracted from his own pre-set game plan. In the future, he and he alone would decide what was or wasn't a good career move for Dorian Yates along the road to being "different."

In November 1986, he returned to Wembley Conference Centre four pounds heavier and scooped the British heavyweight title, but lost the nod for the overall accolade to light-heavyweight Chris Oskys, in what can most politely be termed a controversial decision. As he came offstage, I fully expected Yates' sphinx-like demeanor to explode – and he had ample cause. Dorian just nodded and said quietly, "I'm pissed off with that result." He never uttered another public word about the affair. He had learned another invaluable bodybuilding lesson: It's not good enough to be the best, you have to be the best by a country mile. He retreated to his Birmingham base, not to be heard from for another two years.

It was during the run-in to the 1986 British Championships that I dubbed Dorian Yates "The Shadow." The nickname was sparked as a means of symbolizing his low-profile existence, wherein he emerged without fanfare in sporadic contest apearances to decimate the hopes of his peers before departing the stage and returning to his private Birmingham lair. That modus operandi was to remain in effect throughout his career.

The next year brought more trauma, this time played out away from the glare of the stage spotlight. Just prior to the '86 British Championships, Dorian sustained a hip injury that progressively worsened, increasingly inhibiting his training. By June '87, after eight months of alternative treatment, Yates submitted to surgery for a make-or-break operation. During the same period, he successfully negotiated the purchase of his own training facility, named Temple Gym, in the center of Birmingham.

The surgery proved an immediate and complete success, and by September '87, The Shadow was back with a vengeance, his physique ready for exertions to come and his financial base more secure. He eyed the '88 British Championships, the overall title and the IFBB pro card bequeathed such success. This time, he vowed there would be no mistakes, no room for vacillation. He would quite simply leave the judges with no options but to agree that he was different.

On November 13th, 1988, as the heavyweights rumbled out for battle, my humble pen scrawled the comment "as soon as Dorian Yates walked onstage, it was clear that the rest of the lineup had as much chance as a one-legged man in an ass-kicking contest." Receiving the overall title and accompanying pro card, his 226-pound package was also generally acclaimed the best ever produced in Britain. Abetted by such an adjudication, many urged Dorian to go straight into the pros. The object of all this praise had no wish to join the ranks of those who in one mad rush went from numero uno amateur status and "rose without trace" to become a pro also-ran fiddling about with double-digit placings. The new British champion reflected at the time: "Even though I'm pleased with the progress I've made and the physique I've displayed today, it's a different ball game with the pros, and I've got 18 months of working like a dog before I'll be ready to stand alongside them. I've no wish to run into a contest and make a fool of myself, leaving my career in a cul-de-sac. I want to be a success in the sport of bodybuilding. Besides my own efforts, Debbie has sacrificed too much for me to make a mess of it for us now. Eighteen months takes me to May 1990 and the Night Of Champions, and that's when and where I plan to enter my first pro contest." With this undertaking, The Shadow glided into the background to initiate his singular preparation for the next rung of the competitive ladder, the IFBB professional ranks.

THE ROOKIE PRO

In late 1989, as Dorian Yates prepared for the Night Of Champions, I attempted to garner him some stateside precontest publicity so that he wouldn't arrive in New York as a complete unknown. I wrote about him being a different bodybuilder, a future Mr. Olympia. The following is part of the article I submitted.

Despite the excellence of the physique, the attribute that imbues itself most after any exposure to Dorian Yates, and this applies right from his novice days, is his mental attitude. He has a clinical sense of reality regarding the dimensions of the next hurdle and enjoys an almost spiritual patience in formulating and completing the necessary groundwork. Bodybuilding is littered with the wasted potential of those whose outstanding genetics were not in sync with the intricacies contained within the bodypart that starts at the end of the neck. Dorian Yates is different. In a sport where exaggeration and hyperbole are rampant and every second person you trip over in the gym is training for the Mr. O,

Dorian Yates is a one-off. His career has an almost inevitable consistency to it. No bragging. No boasting to impress others or to give himself confidence. He just sets his sights on the next target, assesses what he has to do and then disappears for the required period to assemble the required goods. His dedication is phenomenal, his training intensity legendary, and although these factors have caused his physique to evolve spectacularly, the inner man remains unchanged, maintaining the same private disposition so apparent when he first so dramatically burst into the sport.

Many interpret this reserved nature for all manner of characteristics; arrogance, aloofness, shyness and lack of confidence are among the front-runners. They're all wrong. The truth is that, unlike many competitors whose bodybuilding exploits are a substitute for some component they feel they've missed out on in life, Dorian Yates, the complete personality, is contented and confident about what he does. Don't look for the chink in his psychological armor responsible for drawing him to the sanctuary of bodybuilding. Ask me to encapsulate the enigma of Dorian Yates and this would be my statement: "Many bodybuilders proclaim that they were born to bodybuild, but Dorian Yates is the first one I've met in over 30 years of my preoccupation for this sport for whom there seems no other explanation or choice. He is so ideally suited for this sport, physically and mentally, that if bodybuilding didn't exist, it's a good bet Dorian Yates would invent it."

The attempt at stateside publicity did not work. I was told by a predecessor at FLEX, "We don't want anything from Britain." (By 1992, Dorian Yates was Mr. Olympia, and I had relocated to Woodland Hills, California, employed by Joe Weider, the publisher of FLEX.)

NEW YORK, NEW YORK

As for Dorian, it wasn't enough that he was an unknown, with no publicity, making his pro debut at the 1990 Night Of Champions, the longest-established pro event apart from the Mr. Olympia. No, he had to promise himself and wife Debbie that if he didn't make the top three, he would there and then quit the sport for good. And he meant it!

Deliberately placing himself in a do-or-die situation allowed him to stoke up the furnace, and this enabled him to be even more severe in the gym. His self-flagellation policy made his task more formidable and also cemented, if there was any doubt, his underdog status.

On May 19, 1990, charged by the fate that awaited him if he failed, the newcomer – referred to as "Dorian Who?" as he walked onstage – stormed to second place behind Mohamed Benaziza. Yates' 228-pound physique was generally commended as the largest accumulation of quality shredded tissue ever displayed proportionately for public consideration. Benaziza may have won the contest, but Dorian Yates was the star of the show. His arrival as a major force was authenticated by Joe Weider whisking the Briton to California for seven days of photography and interview sessions, with the results destined for the pages of FLEX and MUSCLE & FITNESS.

In the fall of 1990, Yates was wooed by the short-lived WBF (World Bodybuilding Federation, an offshoot of Vince McMahon's World Wrestling Federation), who were throwing contract money at leading IFBB pros with all the discretion of Dennis Rodman in a bridal-gown shop. At that time, Dorian didn't have an endorsement deal with anyone. He astonishingly turned down a $200,000-a-year contract from the WBF, such was his commitment to win the Mr. Olympia title.

Dorian returned to the Night Of Champions in May 1991 to stun the Manhattan muscle masses with a physique seven pounds heavier than the year before, displaying improvements to his shape that seemed to defy the laws of genetics. Prominent among his improvements was his back. In 1990, no one

raved about Yates' back; now it was earning comparison with the current Mr. Olympia, Lee Haney. The reason for this "back to front" metamorphosis is quintessential Yates.

Counseled by many witnesses after the 1990 Night Of Champions that he deserved to have beaten Benaziza, Dorian dismissed such verdicts, preferring to regard his satisfaction with his placing at his pro debut. Commenting on Benaziza, he lauded the deep separation displayed in all areas of the Algerian's back and readily stated that he, Dorian, was very much second best in that department. In preparing for the 1991 Night Of Champions, Dorian chose to keep only one photograph as a reminder of his 1990 foray. He had two copies of the image on permanent view, one at his home and one at his gym. It was a back shot – a back shot of Mohamed Benaziza.

With his back development and his first pro victory now in place, here indeed was a contender with the head-to-toe credentials to take on current Mr. Olympia Lee Haney in all departments.

I'M GOING TO DISNEYWORLD

The 1991 Mr. Olympia was staged at the Walt Disney Dolphin Hotel in Orlando, Florida, on September 14. The smart set took the view that, in the four months between the Night Of Champions in May and the Olympia contest, it was impossible for Yates to improve and he would do well to repeat his New York form. Anyway, Lee Haney was unbeatable, especially in view of him carrying the motivational impetus of eclipsing Arnold Schwarzenegger by taking a record eighth Sandow.

One person who later told me that the 1991 Olympia was not a done deal for Lee Haney was Lee Haney. The Awesome One saw the pictures of Yates from the Night Of Champions and realized that he would have to be at his absolute best to guarantee victory and, great champion that he is, Haney did come in at his best to win the contest. But this wasn't before he and Yates produced one of the most electric episodes in bodybuilding history.

For the final callout of the 1991 Mr. Olympia contest, only two protagonists were invited: 240-pound Yates (five quality pounds heavier than in May) and 248-pound Lee Haney in his best-ever shape. In front of a prejudging audience of 3,000 spectators going wild – sections of the crowd were actually stamping their feet – Haney and Yates flexed their all in a titanic struggle during which it took a full four minutes to complete the seven comparisons. When the dust settled, Yates had taken the muscularity round, but the reigning champion won the other three rounds and relegated the Olympia rookie to second. If anyone ever tries to tell you that bodybuilding is not a true sport, just refer them to Haney vs. Yates in Orlando, 1991.

The twosome would never meet again in competition. Lee Haney's legendary career ended that night with his eighth Sandow and a "place in history." On the day the Awesome One took his last step on an Olympia stage, Dorian had taken his first, and by accepting the baton from the eight-time champ, the Englishman was set to carve out a unique Olympia record of his own.

CHAPTER 3

FIVE SANDOWS AND A LEGEND

1992: TO HELSINKI AND BACK

Through his career to this point, Dorian had reveled in the role of underdog, a stance that had taken him to the brink of the Olympia title. The irony is that the 1992 Mr. Olympia (when he actually became the best bodybuilder in the world) occurred on the one occasion when his "David against Goliath" approach sustained a slight blip.

With reigning champion Lee Haney out of the 1992 Olympia picture, Yates was installed as the precontest favorite, and earlier in the year he was confident he could take that rating in his stride. But three days before the contest, he found himself in a strange kind of limbo in regard to his mindset toward the event. It wasn't that he was worried or nervous – it was the exact opposite: He had to constantly remind himself that the contest was imminent. After the press conference, when he saw the other competitors for the first time, he was back in one-track motivational mode.

Yet, he was again entertaining mental gremlins the night before the contest. Was it possible that, out of all the countless bodybuilders on the planet, he could be the best? He asked his wife Debbie, "The best bodybuilder in the world, could it be me?" Within a split-second, he answered his own question, "Somebody's got to be the best . . . why not me?"

After cultivating an underdog persona, his fluctuating state of mind occurred because the true underdogs at the 1992 Mr. Olympia were those challenging him. Did he feel out of character because

A PORTRAIT OF DORIAN YATES   **15**

he couldn't concoct a vision of a big bad bogeyman waiting to ambush him?

The other most spoken-about contender for the Helsinki Olympia was Vince Taylor, who was third right behind Dorian at the '91 Mr. Olympia contest, after which he dominated that year's European tour before nailing down the top spot at the 1992 Arnold Schwarzenegger Classic. Upon arriving in Helsinki, Taylor sustained a freakish eye accident courtesy of a rogue luggage strap with whiplash intentions, mistimed his peak and finished sixth while wearing an eye patch. Lou Ferrigno, after a 17-year absence, made a much-hyped return to competition, but he was never a factor in the contest and finished 12th.

The 1992 Mr. Olympia competition was held in an ice rink (in fact, a hockey match was staged between the prejudging and evening finals). In that frigid setting, Yates, despite some confusing callouts, won quite handily, winning all four rounds. At 242 pounds, he was dry and cut, his arid condition verified by a couple of bouts of cramping. At his moment of victory, the instant of being crowned the best bodybuilder on Earth, Yates punched the air. Backstage, when asked for a comment, he allowed the wry aside, "I suppose I feel pretty good."

The day after being crowned Mr. Olympia, Dorian returned to England with his triumph-symbolizing Sandow to win the English Grand Prix in Nottingham, in front of 2,000 ecstatic countrymen. As a post-mortem to his Olympia victory, he confided that, at 242 pounds, he had dieted down a bit too far and maintained that he could have been as many as seven pounds heavier without any loss of condition. He promised he would not make the same mistake in 1993.

1993: THE NEW LEVEL

While preparing for the 1993 Mr. Olympia contest in Atlanta, Dorian and Debbie struck up a friendship with one of bodybuilding's most prominent couples, Steve Weinberger and Bev Francis, who own Bev Francis Gold's Gym on Long Island in New York. Eleven days out from the contest, Dorian flew to New York, did his final preparation at the Weinbergers' gym and then traveled to Atlanta four days before the contest. He would repeat this ritual for the next four Olympias, and whenever he was in the United States, he made the Weinberger enclave his base.

Two days before the 1993 Mr. Olympia, Yates had never appeared so relaxed in the countdown to a contest. As he flexed in front of his hotel room, it was impossible not to ask why. Hitting a most muscular, he responded, "You'd be friggin' relaxed if you looked like this two days before a show." The defending Mr. O stated that come Saturday, he would weigh 257 pounds, a full 15 pounds heavier than when he won the title in Helsinki a year previously. Explaining the startling metamorphosis, Dorian said: "Knowing that Lee Haney would not be at last year's Olympia, I figured that my closest rivals would be Shawn Ray and Vince Taylor, neither of whom weigh more than 210 pounds. I went for condition at the expense of size, overdieted and came in too light. This year, I've just concentrated on being the best I can be."

Yates also confided that the reaction to his '92 win by some sections of the bodybuilding community vexed him. Many wrote him off as a one-time Mr. Olympia. Proof of his simmering irritation was provided by a poster that adorned his gym in Birmingham, England. The poster's inscription read "1993 Mr. Olympia, Atlanta. To all the disbelievers, Kiss My Ass."

The champ may not have been too consumed by his rivals, but the reverse was certainly not true. The leading contenders had heard the rumors of an unbelievable Yates guest-posing in New York in July and several of them, including Paul Dillett and Flex Wheeler, had a pre-Olympia sight of the

sensational photos of the 269-pound Yates that eventually appeared in the December '93 issue of FLEX. Nobody can say they weren't warned.

A couple of minutes after 2 PM on September 11, 1993, Dorian Yates strode onto the stage of Atlanta's Civic Auditorium and in one fell swoop redefined bodybuilding criteria. At 257 pounds, he was the heaviest Mr. Olympia ever, but compounding the size factor was tissue-paper-thin skin, full muscularity, detail in places where other people didn't have places and great proportions. Samir Bannout, 1983 Mr. Olympia, spoke for many when he said, "Dorian was first, second and third." The phrase "Dorian has taken the sport to a new level" was freely used. Indeed, such was Dorian's supremacy that the judges saw no need to call him out for a muscularity comparison. It was IFBB Pro Division Chairman Wayne DeMilia who "for the audience" decided to call the comparison of Yates with Flex Wheeler and Shawn Ray, who finished second and third respectively.

Wheeler, who came into the contest on a roll and was the favorite of many after winning four shows out of four in his rookie year, had no complaint with the verdict: "I couldn't have handled Dorian today. He was a mule in shape."

As for the main man himself, in the sanctuary of his dressing room, he explained what winning his second Sandow meant: "After last year's result, when I was too light, my goal for this year was to achieve something not only for myself but for the sport as a whole. I wanted to set a new standard for competitive bodybuilding." That he had surely accomplished, for in the wake of his triumph, the sport went size crazy. In the 1993 Mr. Olympia lineup, only Yates and Paul Dillett of the top ten exceeded 250 pounds, six of the top ten would break the 250-pound mark by 1996.

1994: AGAINST ALL ODDS

In February 1994, Dorian Yates weighed 295 pounds and was stronger and harder than he had ever been at that weight. After his "new level" triumph of 1993, he was enthusiastically looking forward to dramatically improving on that form at the 1994 Mr. Olympia seven months later. As befits someone of such prodigious wing span, Dorian was flying high.

In July of 1994, two months out from the September 10 Mr. Olympia contest in Atlanta, Dorian Yates felt like a stricken Lancaster bomber flying back to base with one engine gone, his navigational instruments shot to pieces and a fire in the hold. He was still in the air, with the landing site just over the horizon; the trick now was to generate enough power to find his way home and glide successfully onto the runway without sustaining any further damage. How had he arrived at such a perilous position?

The nightmare began on March 7, when Yates tore a ligament that impinged on the rotator cuff in his left shoulder joint during a warm-up set of decline presses. Doctors told him to completely cease training and undergo corrective surgery, a course of action that would keep him out of the gym for at least two months. It seemed he would not be able to defend his title. As a last resort, in mid-April, he received cortisone-injection treatment that eased the pain and dissipated the inflammation quite dramatically. The treatment afforded the shoulder joint a better range of movement, but he was only able to handle much lighter weights than previously had been the case. He was still unable to do any pressing movements – chest or delt work – until the shoulder was operated on. Dorian made an appointment for surgery in October, a month after his scheduled flexing date in Atlanta. During the interim, there was the ever-present threat that the shoulder-joint inflammation could flare up again at any time.

In early April, still in the throes of sorting out his shoulder problems, he tore the vastus muscle in his left thigh and was prevented from training legs for five weeks. After that period, his leg work was confined to a high-rep regimen on selected exercises until the contest.

On July 12, less than nine weeks before the competition, just as Dorian thought he'd overcome the worst year of his training life, a searing pain shot up his arm as he repped out on barbell rows with 405 pounds. He said: "I dropped the weight immediately and knew the damage was serious. I instantly thought the whole biceps had detached from the bone. I was devastated. I thought my 1994 Olympia bid, maybe my career, was over."

Knowledge of Dorian's quad and shoulder mishaps had been privy only to his inner circle, but reports that he'd suffered a serious biceps tear swept through the bodybuilding community. Dorian downplayed the injury, saying that he'd merely strained some muscle fibers in his forearm. Nevertheless, the biceps was torn, although the tendon had not detached from the bone. The prognosis was that it would heal over time. But time was one commodity that Yates didn't have: The Olympia was two months away.

Taking stock of his wounded physique and facing the thought of Olympia withdrawal made Dorian realize how much the contest meant to him. It had changed his life, as well of those of his wife Debbie and son Lewis.

Looking back, Dorian recalls his mindset: "For 12 days, I was forced to consider whether I could go on or not. I assessed the situation, and felt I had come too far not to pursue things to the limit of my capabilities. I figured I'd proceed with a restricted training regimen – go with what I'd got and give it my all. Two weeks or so out, if my physique had deteriorated to a point where I felt I wouldn't be good enough to win, or if I sustained a further injury, I'd drop out. I just couldn't give up; that course wasn't open. I had to go the point of knowing absolutely that it wasn't possible rather than second-guessing that it wasn't possible.

"After that period of inactivity, my back and biceps routines were decimated. For back, bent-over rows and deadlifts were out, and I was restricted to four exercises: Nautilus pullovers, hyperextensions, very light parallel-grip pulldowns and very light Hammer Strength machine rows. For the latter two exercises, my range of motion [due to the biceps damage] was restricted to two-thirds – from the fully contracted point to two-thirds extension of the arms.

"For biceps, all I could do for the last five weeks of my preparation were standing dumbbell curls and concentration curls, and, even then, the weights were ridiculously light. I started out with 10-pound dumbbells, then progressed through 15s and 20s, so that for the two weeks prior to the contest I was using 30-pound dumbbells. What a beast!"

"I dug down deep and asked myself, 'Do you have the heart and the balls to fight back from this? Are you a true champion, Yates?' "

On September 10, 1994, the Lancaster bomber glided in to a safe and successful landing. Dorian Yates proved himself a true champion and a true warrior by winning his third Sandow trophy against odds no previous champion had endured.

1995: RESPECT

Dorian Yates is a tough guy, the kind who would ask for venison after watching a screening of Bambi. But as befits someone who carries such a low bodyfat percentage at contest time, he can prove to be thin-skinned on some issues. One issue that had been simmering under his almost translucent contest-day skin since the commencement of his Olympia reign was the matter of respect. As Dorian saw it, certain segments of the bodybuilding press (not the fans) had just not given him his proper due following three Olympia wins. And even after the trauma of 1994, when he limped into the contest with the baggage of three serious injuries and still took the title, the press didn't get it. They didn't get Dorian. (Others did. Mike Francois, for instance, said of Dorian's '94 win, "Who else but Dorian would have gone through that and still showed up, never mind showed up good enough to win?")

Why didn't some sections of the press get Dorian? Well, for self-proclaimed gonzo journalists in search of lurid copy, Dorian can be as productive as a fifth amendment plea. Personally, that's always been the attraction: What makes this "different" bodybuilder tick? Yates ticks to a rhythm very different from that measured by the standard bodybuilding clock.

That standard clock accepts that bodybuilding has always been an arena in which extreme hyperbole has been the norm: A 19" arm miraculously becomes a 21" arm, and outlandish claims of poundages lifted spring to life via a creative force that makes the Immaculate Conception seem passé. Yates has never felt the urge to embellish the dimensions of his stock in trade. Indeed, he's prone to do exactly the opposite. It's a paradox that in the most visual sport on earth (bodybuilding contests are actually decided by the visual image presented), it has never been the custom to just let the physiques do the talking. A policy of lying low is shunned in favor of lying as high as one's calcium-loaded back teeth will allow.

During his emergence from unknown to multiple Mr. Olympia, experienced ears waited for Dorian Yates to overstate his case, and the lack of decibel disturbance emanating from his lips seems to have been interpreted by some as proof that he had less than a lot to shout about. Surely he should be bellowing from the nearest Gold's Gym rooftop, "I am the greatest."

By and large, the magazines couldn't figure out where Yates was coming from when it came to dealing with his shadowy machinations. And, hey, Mr. Olympias surely don't come from Birmingham, England, do they? . . . and "Schwarzenegger help us," they surely don't stay in Birmingham!

The fact that Yates is the first man ever to win the Mr. Olympia while living outside the USA should offer a strong clue that he is indeed a different bodybuilder. A different bodybuilder who in the "I've told you a million times, don't exaggerate!" world of bodybuilding has always been underestimated.

So as 1994 gave way to 1995, Dorian Yates was concerned with the subject of respect. Of his 1994 travails, the smart set fostered the triple deflatory theory that Flex Wheeler wasn't there (he was recovering from his near-fatal car crash of June '94), the champ has one hand on the Sandow anyway, and Yates' Weider contract somehow served as a passport to the title. Again, he wasn't being given respect, the respect due a true champion who had drawn upon every reserve of his Churchillian heritage as he persevered against horrendous odds and whipped himself into winning shape.

In 1994, Yates was admittedly not at his best, but he was still the best bodybuilder onstage that day. No one, not even runner-up Shawn Ray, disagreed with that view on the night of Yates' threepeat. It was only as time screwed with memory that the doubters started to rewrite the facts. And so, as he mapped out his approach to the 1995 Olympia showdown in Atlanta on September 9, Dorian Yates declared war. The spoils of this war represented more than a fourth Sandow – the Brit wanted respect.

Fifteen minutes before the prejudging of the 1995 Mr. Olympia, Dorian's mood of open warfare was exemplified by the banter taking place in his dressing room. As he was oiled up by Steve Weinberger, Yates fired off military metaphors: "In 1993, I showed up with a bazooka. Last year, I felt like I had one arm tied behind my back. Today, I'm ready to launch an intercontinental missile."

This is my "as it happened" notepad impression of the 255-pound Yates who appeared onstage that day: Skin like tissue paper. Traps look as if they have the capacity to render him deaf. Back, upper and lower, is sensational in every respect: width, thickness and detail. Side triceps pose is a masterpiece that he's made into a Broadway production number. Thighs have more sweep than before. Calves? Yates wrote the book on calves. In muscle thickness, he's in a class of his own. Today's combination of size, proportion, shape and condition makes this his best-ever form.

The judges gave the champion firsts across the board. No one disputed the win. Yates had followed the war of attrition of '94 with a 1995 blitzkrieg.

1996: HOME AND DRY IN THE WINDY CITY

The 1996 Mr. Olympia contest staged at Chicago's Arie Crown Theatre on September 21 witnessed the introduction of drug testing for diuretics. As dawn broke on the morning of the contest, Dorian Yates knew that a sense of the floodgates having been opened was swirling around the Olympia weekend. The previous evening, the venue had hosted a modern-day rendition of Chicago's St. Valentine's Day Massacre as the other three defending Olympia champions (Fitness diva Mia Finnegan, Masters supremo Sonny Schmidt and Ms. O queen Lenda Murray) were swept from their thrones in a tidal wave of change. Now, the question being asked was would Bloody Friday extend into Bloody Saturday?

For Dorian, there was never a doubt that he would fall victim to the bloodletting that had befallen his 1995 Olympia compatriots. He came to the Windy City loaded for bear of the Chicago variety: He was there to win, and no competitor or newly instituted testing procedure would stand in his way. His confidence was merited, as his 257-pound package was rock hard and drier than a Jackie Mason monologue.

The latter aspect particularly pleased Dorian, who looked upon the diuretic test as an opportunity to prove a point. Over the years, his "big and freaky" status has also carried the inference by those who wish to talk behind the Yates lats that his physique is reliant on drugs. To his detractors, Dorian says, "They overlook the work I do in the gym year-round. I diet down properly for a contest – losing a couple of pounds a week – and am at the weight I want to be two weeks out from a contest. I'm not one of those guys who has to drop ten pounds in the week before a contest. The test allowed me to prove that diuretics are not necessary to get into great condition." By now, the preciseness of Yates' planning and attention to detail was being increasingly recognized. That fastidiousness had been in place since day one, back in 1983.

The 1983 version of Yates already realized – as any natural would in respect of his chosen sport, things come easily to the gifted – that he had good genetics, and that with application, perseverance and a burning will to succeed, he would advance more rapidly than his peers. Furthermore, he had the mental wherewithal to know without having to debate the issue – it's called instinct – that progress would be faster if he programmed his advancement in step-by-step increments rather than by means of unrealistic and spirit-destroying quantum leaps.

Consequently, he turned away – in truth, he never even looked in that direction – from what his Birmingham gym contemporaries of 1983 were doing: The 21-year-old was repping to a beat of a different and more scientific drum. It was a drumbeat that urged his competitive spirit to seek a rival of equal merit. He had to find an foe, and he did: The Dorian Yates who became his bodybuilding enemy stared back at him from the gym mirror at the conclusion of every training session. He would scan his mirror image and – as he still does – criticize what he saw: "Your legs are crap, Yates!" "You gotta bring that back up." If he ever let up on the Yates in the mirror, if he ever told his reflection "You're OK," then progress would cease.

In those circumstances was born and nurtured a subjective intensity of effort that focused inward. Refusing to be distracted by what anybody else was doing, his concentration was targeted solely on making Dorian Yates the best he could be. The duality of effort and introversion never bordered on the unhealthy: It was a perfect state for "Dorian Yates: Bodybuilder." On the outside, he was cool, but within was a white-hot furnace of controlled energy that kept its owner warm and secure in the unconceited knowledge that he was becoming increasingly "different" and that he was able to overcome all hurdles put in front of him. As he took possession of his fifth Sandow, Dorian Yates was not to know that the most threatening hurdle he had ever encountered might bar his way to a sixth.

CHAPTER 4

THE ULTIMATE WARRIOR

For the 1996 Mr. Olympia contest, Dorian had been so consumed by being as dry as possible that he had "overdone things" and come in a little flat and, at 257 pounds, somewhat lighter than he could have been. His 1997 game plan was to return to his normal fullness and weigh around 265 pounds, which would mark his heaviest-ever contest weight.

By the spring of 1997, the five-time champ was experiencing his best-ever offseason. He had never been stronger and eagerly looked forward to defending his Olympia crown in Long Beach, California, on September 19. There was just one niggling problem. Throughout the previous year, he'd been having difficulties with his left elbow, which kept swelling up. A specialist examined the elbow and said the inflammation was a buildup of scar tissue caused by years of stress due to working out. He told Dorian there was a fairly simple arthroscopic surgical procedure to remove the scar tissue, and that it would involve a few weeks of rehabilitation and no training. Dorian made a mental date to have the surgery in October after the Olympia. To alleviate the inflammation, he regularly took small amounts of aspirin.

In mid-June, Yates picked up a cold, and it hung around for a couple of weeks before developing into a severe chest infection. He felt run down and lacking in energy. Then on June 27, he suffered a small tear to his right thigh while doing leg extensions and couldn't train legs for three weeks.

HOSPITALIZED

While Dorian was recovering from the thigh tear, he began to feel very lethargic and completely drained of energy. If he stood up suddenly, he felt dizzy, and a couple of times thought he was going to faint. On the morning of August 1, Yates started his normal 30 minutes of cardio on the stationary bike he has in his home. He felt totally exhausted within 15 minutes, but told himself he had to keep going, because the Olympia was less than eight weeks away. After 20 minutes, he was close to collapse and had to stop.

An ashen-faced Dorian lurched into the kitchen. Debbie saw him and blurted out, "What the hell's wrong with you?" Dorian started coughing up blood and was rushed straight to the hospital. The doctors who diagnosed internal bleeding had trouble correcting the problem. Over the next three days, Dorian received three transfusions, totaling about 10 pints of blood.

The first night Dorian was in the hospital, Debbie sat at home with 13-year-old Lewis and thought, Why Dorian, why him again? Why is God constantly testing him? For Dorian, there's always a mountain to climb.

Dorian kept telling the doctors, "I have to train!" "You're not training or leaving that bed until you're OK," Debbie insisted. Nevertheless, their 14-year relationship had taught her that however bad the situation appeared, Dorian needed to keep his focus on the Olympia. She made sure he kept to his diet by cooking all his meals at home and bringing them to the hospital. Afterwards, she was to say, "If I could have smuggled in an Olympic barbell set, he would have let me."

Eventually, it was discovered that the aspirin Dorian had been taking for his elbow inflammation had caused a small tear in the wall of his stomach, which led to the internal bleeding.

Because of the amount of blood he'd lost, Dorian's hemoglobin count was so low that he was nearly anemic. The hemoglobin index represents the capacity to transport oxygen in the bloodstream. A normal hemoglobin level is somewhere between 12 and 16. Dorian has his blood tested regularly and knew his normal level was 17, but it was down to 10 by the time he was admitted to the hospital.

He left the hospital on Monday morning, August 4, and was told to take it easy for a few weeks. Dorian asked the doctors what they thought about him training again, and they said it was up to him. Even though he was very tired, Dorian felt he could still win the Olympia.

A couple of weeks after leaving the hospital, Dorian's hemoglobin level was back in the normal zone at 12, but he lacked energy and was weaker than normal because oxygen just wasn't being supplied in sufficient quantities to his blood. By the Olympia, it was up to 14; short of his customary count, but he no longer felt tired.

Upon his return home, Debbie told Dorian: "Take it easy; leave the cardio alone for a while. Thank God you've worked so hard and your physique's in such great condition. You did all the work before you started dieting. Now all you have to do is lower the calories and get sharper. You don't have to bust your backside in the gym." She reinforced the message: "Beggars can't be choosers. You're not 100%, so you can't put out 100%. If you want to do the Olympia, you have to compromise and play the cards dealt you."

HANGING BY A THREAD

Three weeks out from the Olympia, Dorian was doing the pullover portion of a pullover-and-press for triceps. He remembers the fateful moment: "I felt something go bang in my left elbow, followed by the most enormous pain. I knew straight away the triceps had gone. It was much more painful than

A PORTRAIT OF DORIAN YATES 27

Post 1997 Photo Shoot

when I tore my biceps [nine weeks prior to the '94 Mr. Olympia]. In fact, it was so painful that I think I went into shock, because it was as if, after the initial agony, I couldn't feel anything. I thought, That's it, no Olympia. Everything I've done this year has been for nothing — it's over. My whole upper arm swelled up, the triceps was totally distorted, and my arm was bruised down to the wrist by the next day. It was the only time in my life that I've thought, I can't fight this!"

With so much swelling, a diagnosis couldn't be given immediately, but it eventually proved to be a full-blown tear. Yates' triceps tendon was torn three-quarters of the way off the bone, so it was attached along only a quarter of its length. Dorian's triceps and Olympia hopes were literally hanging by a thread.

The night of the injury was the lowest Debbie had ever seen Dorian. He told her, "It's over Deb, I can't beat this one!" The next morning, the first thing Debbie said to him was "You haven't worked your arse off for a year to sit at home on Olympia day. You can do it." Dorian quietly replied, "I know I can."

Explaining the overnight turnaround, Dorian says, "By the next morning, my mind began to fight back. I thought, Even though my training from here on is gonna be all screwed up, I'm in shape; I can do it. I just have to grit it out for three weeks. I adopted the same attitude I had with the biceps tear in 1994: 'Don't dare give up until it's absolutely clear you can't compete. Otherwise, you'll spend the rest of your life thinking, Could I have done it?"

His main worry was the uncertainty. Would the swelling and bruising disperse before the Olympia? What would the triceps look like? Yates was prepared to go through all the discomfort and suspense, but there was no guarantee that it wouldn't be in vain.

In those last three weeks, he couldn't do any pressing movements, and even most pulling movements had to be done very carefully with light weights. For chest, he was restricted to the pec-deck; for delts, just lateral raises. The only bodypart he could train properly was legs. He didn't practice any posing for those three weeks, because even the action of flexing his left triceps could lead to inflammation of the elbow.

Even pulling on his pants was difficult. Debbie says, "Those last three weeks, I was the one who pulled his pants up. It bothered him to be that helpless. I said, 'Shut up, if you can't do it and I can, what's your problem? As long as it's me pulling up your pants, I don't care.' Watching him those last three weeks ripped my heart apart. I saw how much his body was hurting. I felt his pain. I knew he was depressed and totally frustrated within himself, but he didn't show it, didn't force his anguish on anyone. He'd cheerfully ask me how I was, how Lewis was doing, act normally, even though he must have been crying inside. I couldn't grab him and hold him and cry on his shoulder because he needed all the positive input he could get. It was only after the contest that I crashed."

On Friday, September 12, seven days before the Olympia, Dorian and Debbie arrived in California. The bruising and swelling in his triceps had disappeared. He could compete without the injury standing out like a red flag. Since tearing the triceps, he had lived with constant uncertainty and the fear that it would suddenly break down again and swell up. On Saturday, September 13, he was drying himself after a shower when a searing pain shot through his left triceps. Dorian gasped, "No, not now!" He immediately applied an ice pack and, after a few hours, it became clear the triceps wasn't going to swell up again. He was now almost paranoid about anything involving the triceps and the shower incident underlined the need to desist from practicing posing. He had to save everything for the competition.

TOUGHING IT OUT

The 1997 Mr. Olympia contest was played out over a two-day format: Friday night was prejudging; Saturday night was the finals. At 266 pounds, Dorian came in at his heaviest contest weight ever, but still remained as hard as a rock and was fuller, particularly in his thighs and delts. During the prejudging, he was at the edge of exhaustion – he'd hardly slept for days – and his thoughts were consumed by his triceps. Constantly, he told himself, Be very careful when you hit a pose; don't squeeze hard with that left arm. Normally, his thoughts during prejudging were along the lines of Yeah! Let's get down to business. This time, he was thinking, I hope to hell they don't call me again, I'd rather just stay back here. With the prejudging over, he felt a wave of relief because all that was left was the next day's finals, involving a three-minute posing routine and the posedown.

After the prejudging, Dorian knew he had a lock on the title. As he tried to relax in his hotel room on the morning of the finals, he had no doubts that his 1997 campaign represented the supreme example of Team Yates in action. "Debbie was the one who pulled me through. If it wasn't for her, I wouldn't have been able to go on. There's no way I would have been able to do what I did without Debbie being there for me every minute of each day, ready to say, 'Come on, you can do it.' I've always loved and appreciated her for what she means to me, but, if possible, this year has brought us even closer together. We went through it together . . . alone!"

As for Debbie, her most recurring memory of 1997 is of Dorian lying in a hospital bed as she told him, "It's not about me loving Dorian the bodybuilder, I love Dorian the person. Whatever happens to you affects me and Lewis." She adds, "He knows that I would never tell him not to compete. When the day comes, it will be his decision and the right one. He has his own destiny, one that Lewis and I are included in, but one he has to decide for himself."

Reflecting on the tribulations of the 13 weeks prior to the 1997 Olympia, Dorian asserted: "Coming through that period confirms how important the offseason is. That's when you make all your gains. I proved that having 14 years of intensity workouts in your training log builds a density of muscle that is not going to disappear overnight. I got away with doing a fraction of the work I planned to do in the last few weeks and still came in bigger and just as hard. A lot of people will say that my experiences prove that I train too heavy, too hard, and that I'm maybe crazy. I say I train intelligently, but I also train with a passion; I'm constantly walking a fine line as I explore the limits of my capabilities. I don't take the view that I don't need to improve, that I'm good enough to keep winning the Olympia, so why risk injury? Maybe that's the smart way to do it, but for me that approach lacks passion. If I'm gonna do the Olympia, I've got to give of my best in the gym to be at my best onstage. That means pushing myself to the limit. If you don't overstep your limits, how do you know what your limits are?"

For the finals, Dorian filled out to 270 pounds and swept to a straight-firsts victory. As Yates clutched his sixth Sandow and stood onstage with Joe Weider on the evening of Saturday, September 20, the 2,500 who packed Long Beach's Terrace Theater didn't know that they had just witnessed the ultimate blood-and-guts performance by a man whose spirit and tenacity refused to wilt in the face of the most intense pressure. He stood before them as the sport's ultimate warrior.

THE LAST TIME

Nobody knew it then, but he also stood before them for the last time as a competitor.

The damaged triceps was operated on in New York on October 28, 1997, but healing was slower than expected. By the summer of 1998, he still couldn't train at 100% capacity. He realized his body needed more rest and decided to withdraw from defending his title.

The news shook the bodybuilding world. Dorian's abdication created new opportunities for his competitors, but most thought his respite would be short-lived. It looked like Dorian would just take a year off, then come back in dramatic fashion to rule again in 1999.

The great comeback was not to be, however. In mid-September, only a month before the '98 Mr. Olympia, Dorian made the most difficult decision of his bodybuilding career. He announced his retirement. He had fulfilled his dreams – there were no fresh fields to conquer. Like all great warriors, there were no tears, no regrets: He knew it was time. The decision had been made.

In the final chapter of this book, Dorian talks about enjoying "a degree of good fortune" along his road to immortality. The greater truth is that it was bodybuilding's good fortune to have Dorian Yates as its standard-bearer at a time when the sport experienced a period of explosive growth. Bodybuilding has rarely seen a man with the nobility, courage, integrity and excellence of the six-time Mr. Olympia. The sport has been enhanced and blessed by Dorian's presence, and he will be sorely missed from the competitive stage. The portrait of Dorian Yates is one that is drawn with unique and extraordinary qualities, reflecting a man of special drive and character. He really was a "different" bodybuilder, and there truly will never be another quite like Dorian Yates.

Dorian's Strength and Support – Debbie Yates

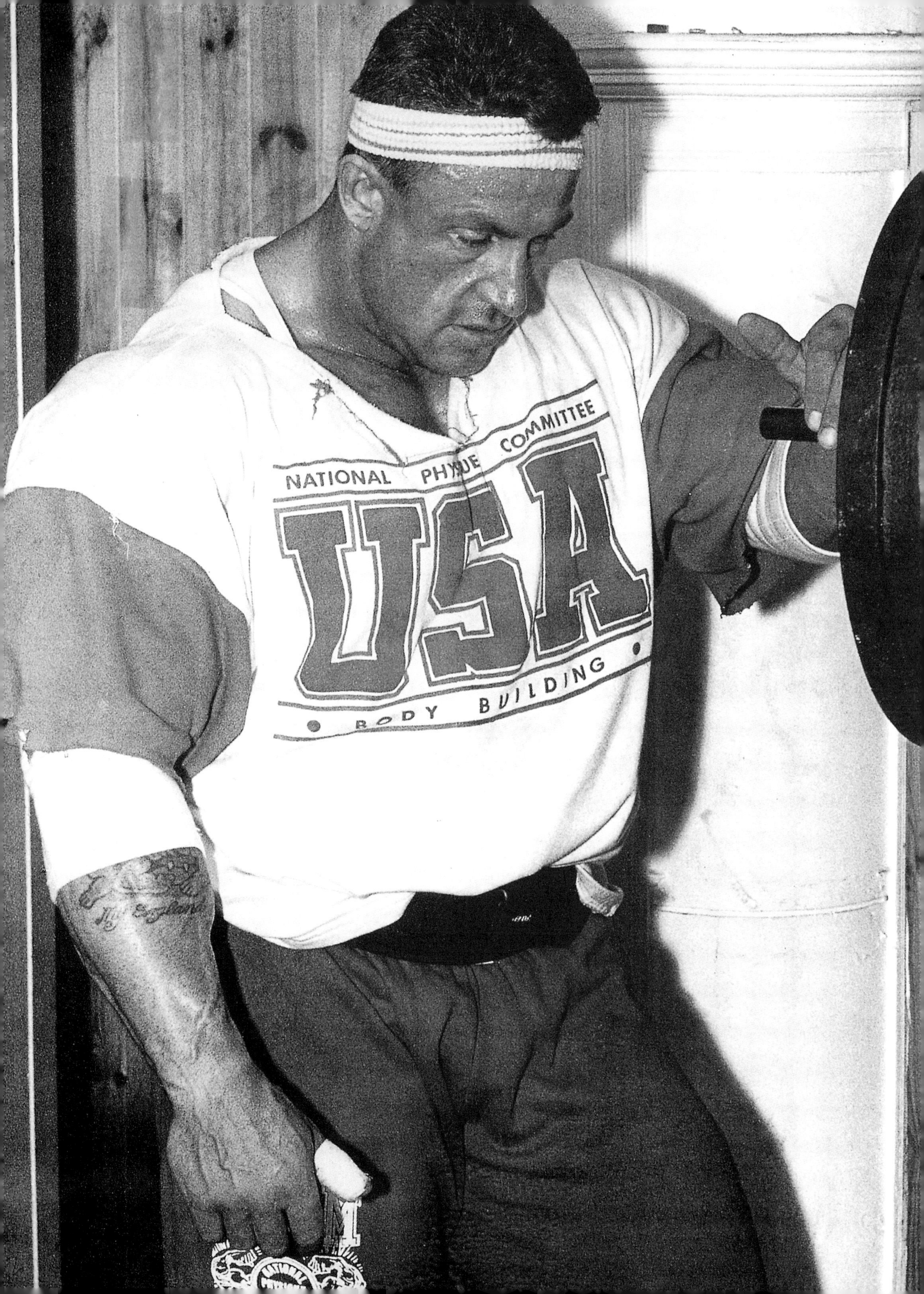
NATIONAL PHYSIQUE COMMITTEE
USA
BODY BUILDING

CHAPTER 5

RECUPERATION:
Bodybuilding's Big Secret

The most abused aspect of the bodybuilding jigsaw puzzle is that of recuperation. That is why I decided to start the instruction section of this book by underlining how imperative an understanding of the recuperation process is to bodybuilding success.

As I progressed through my first two years of serious training, I became increasingly aware of how common it was to overlook the subject of recuperation. I trained among bodybuilders who were training twice a day, six days a week, and who complained about lack of progress and being burned out. It was clear that they were training too often and not allowing sufficient recuperation to take place. To me, bodybuilding is a case of studying and learning from cause and effect. You train because you want to get big, and essentially the muscle-building process occurs in the following three-stage sequence: stimulation; recovery; growth.

The stimulation stage is accomplished by putting a training stress on the body. Then begins the recovery phase. Once the recovery phase is complete, muscle growth occurs. Only after muscle growth has taken place is it time to train those particular muscles again. If you don't allow time for full recuperation between workouts, you'll cease to build muscle, which is the complete opposite of the philosophy of bodybuilding.

All thoughts regarding recuperation filter down into one bodybuilding reality: During the recuperation phase, an individual muscle group responds to an overload of stress by getting stronger, so that it is better able to meet that same level of stress the next time it is asked. Of course, the intention of bodybuilding is to keep increasing that level of stress so that the muscle is consistently forced to grow to meet an escalating demand.

While that muscle-building fundamental seems clear on paper, bodybuilding's most common mistake is overtraining, which can be translated as "allowing insufficient recuperation time." Falling into the trap of not allowing sufficient recuperation time leads not just to lack of progress, but in fact a regression in levels of muscle and strength.

An apt analogy follows: If you briskly rub sandpaper on the palm of your hand for a brief but intense moment, you will break the skin. In a day or two, that skin will heal to form a callus. That's the body's way of making itself better able to combat the next bout of sandpaper friction. However, if you were to rub your palm with sandpaper every day (even with lesser intensity than the original manner) before the skin had healed and the callus had formed, you would disrupt the skin even more. The end result would be that the skin would grow even more scarred and tender, and it would not be able to deal with any level of sandpaper application.

THE WHOLE STORY

When it comes to the subject of recuperation, many bodybuilders think in terms of recovery of individual bodyparts, but recuperation should also be considered as it applies to the body as a whole entity.

The recuperation of the whole physiological system should be the prime concern. For example, the precept that it takes three days for each bodypart to recover from a workout can logically lead to the assumption that you can train (i.e., on a one bodypart per day basis) each and every day.

The forgotten factor within the construction of such a program is that, for optimum recovery, the body's overall physiological and nervous system needs whole days at a time free from gym exertions. That's why I always advocate programs formulated around training only three or four times per week. Such a workout frequency offers not only a mental break, but the physical bonus of allowing your whole nervous system adequate time to recover and regroup for the next assault. As will be covered later, the overtraining syndrome doesn't manifest itself primarily in muscle fatigue, but as a general breakdown of the nervous system.

If your workouts constitute 100% all-out efforts – which they need to if you want to make the required progress – then you must have days free of weight-training activity, otherwise you won't be allowing appropriate recuperation time. The actual body building process takes place out of the gym, not in the gym. Spend too much time in the gym, and you won't grow!

A QUESTION OF TIME

In terms of required intensity, bodybuilding is a sport unlike any other. I've spoken with many track & field athletes, who have been amazed that I work out in the gym for only four hours or so a week. To build the sort of size I have, they assume that my workout quota would be similar to their four-hours-a-day, six-days-a-week schedules.

What is overlooked is that the track & field athletes' programs call for a repetitive regimen of practice. In contrast, when a bodybuilder is in the gym, he's not practicing, he is – or should be – competing. A bodybuilder applies maximum stress throughout his time in the gym, while athletes in other sports tend to follow programs that incorporate a gradual buildup of intensity and periods of just ticking over, even though they are putting in a lot of hours of effort.

A PORTRAIT OF DORIAN YATES 35

Dorian and family relaxing away from the gym

Like fellow athletes from other sports, many bodybuilders (who quite rightly look upon themselves as athletes) feel that as they develop, so should the length of their training sessions. Volume work is not the key to bodybuilding success!

As you grow bigger and stronger, it is possible to put increasing levels of stress on your musculature. However, the body's ability to recuperate from increased inputs of stress doesn't grow at the same rate as strength and muscle improvements. Consider the beginner with a 13" arm who starts out by curling 40 pounds. After a few years, he has an 18" arm capable of curling 160 pounds. That represents a 400% increase in stress input and strength. The body's ability to recuperate from that stress won't have increased as dramatically; it's increased by maybe 50%. The other factor to be taken into account is that the intensity of effort required to fatigue a 18" arm is much greater than that which is required to fatigue a 13" arm. So, with strength increases not being commensurate with the powers of recuperation, plus the greater intensity of effort that is required in order to fatigue a muscle group made stronger by years of effort, the reality is that it will take the 18" arm longer to recover than the 13" arm. A 13" arm can probably recover in a couple of days, while an 18" arm will take five to six days to fully recuperate.

Your route to muscular progress is to increase your intensity of training, but as that intensity increases, it follows that the stress upon your recuperative powers is that much greater. The conundrum - for purposes of recuperation - is that as the intensity of effort increases, the frequency of effort should decrease.

From 1987 through 1991, I was hitting each bodypart once every five days. As I got stronger and was able to exert an increasing degree of intensity, I decided to cut back to working each bodypart every six days, beginning in 1992. In 1994, I began to train each bodypart once every seven days. The other turndown in volume was that I began to do only one main set per exercise in 1992 as compared to two or three sets previously. I was spending less time in the gym, but making more progress than I ever had. Correctly fine-tuning the required individual balance between intensity and recuperation is the route to consistent progress.

AN OPEN AND SHUT-EYE CASE

Obtaining adequate sleep is an indispensable piece of the recuperation jigsaw. During sleep, the body replenishes depleted reserves more quickly, repairs the nervous system and releases its own stores of growth hormone.

I usually sleep eight hours each night, plus another 1 1/2 to 2 hours in the afternoon. As a pro bodybuilder, I can plan for an afternoon nap, even though I realize that such a program is not practical for a majority of weight-trainers. I've found that an afternoon nap, in addition to eight hours per night, is more beneficial than trying to sleep for 10 hours at a stretch. That tends to make me even more drowsy the next day. In a lot of cultures, it is accepted as natural to sleep in the afternoon, as energy reserves are low at that time.

If you feel fresh and energetic during the day, then you are getting enough sleep. If not, your instinct will usually be able to tell you whether you need more or less sleep. Never think that you can get by on the minimum of sleep. Recuperation is fundamental to building muscle, and adequate sleep is fundamental to recuperation.

NUTRITION AND RECUPERATION

There's no single magic nutritional item that will help boost recuperation. A well-balanced nutritious diet is part of the whole "training-recuperation-growth" chain. As explained more fully in Chapter Seventeen, diet should be split 50-55% carbohydrate, 30% protein and 15-20% fat.

Within the context of recuperation, carbohydrate fulfills a very dynamic role. Carbs are essential for restoring the body's glycogen reserves. Glycogen is paramount in the recuperation/muscle-building process. In the postworkout period, the body is crying out for the replacement of depleted glycogen stores. So much so, that during the postworkout phase the body actually releases enzymes that aid the storage of glycogen. That's why I immediately have a liquid carb drink after a workout, which starts the muscle-recuperation ball rolling straight away. Then, within two hours of the workout, I eat my highest calorie meal of the day; this influx of nutrients acts as another key recuperation booster. The liquid carbs and the high-calorie meal are much more beneficial for my body's needs when I'm in the immediate postworkout state than if I ingest them at some other time of day.

As regards supplements that aid the recuperation process, the main ones would be vitamin B and vitamin C. Vitamin B facilitates the absorption of protein and carbs, thus aiding the recuperation process. Vitamin C helps strengthen the immune system. Colds, sore throats and infections are common symptoms of the immune system's breakdown and are usually byproducts of the overtraining syndrome.

OVERTRAINING: SYMPTOMS AND CURE

Following are the classic signs of not recuperating fully, i.e. overtraining.

1) General feeling of tiredness
2) Irritability
3) Trouble sleeping
4) Loss of appetite
5) Joint aches
6) Thick head and nausea
7) Not being in a positive frame of mind

A combination of some or all of these symptoms will result in a lack of enthusiasm in regard to approaching your next workout. That frame of mind is not conducive to gathering your forces for workouts that require 100% effort. If you are serious about making improvements, a hunger for training is a prerequisite for entering the gym. Once you hit the recuperation wall, the only cure – apart from not hitting it in the first place – is to stay out of the gym completely until the genuine feeling of hunger returns.

While you are recuperating, analyze your workout schedule and streamline it, either by cutting back on training frequency or the prescribed workload for each session. Adhering to your new schedule, give it all you've got when the overtraining symptoms dissipate and you strongly feel you are ready to resume your path to growth.

If you're stubborn about ignoring the signs of overtraining, your workouts will become counterproductive. You'll lose size and strength, and you'll feel lousy too. In my early bodybuilding days, I used to think it was wimpish to throttle back when my body was screaming for a couple of days out of the gym. I now recognize that such a kamikaze spirit is self-destructive. I've learned from those mistakes, and I realized that improvement is enhanced not by training harder and longer, but by training smarter. Think smart and recuperate to accumulate.

A PORTRAIT OF DORIAN YATES 39

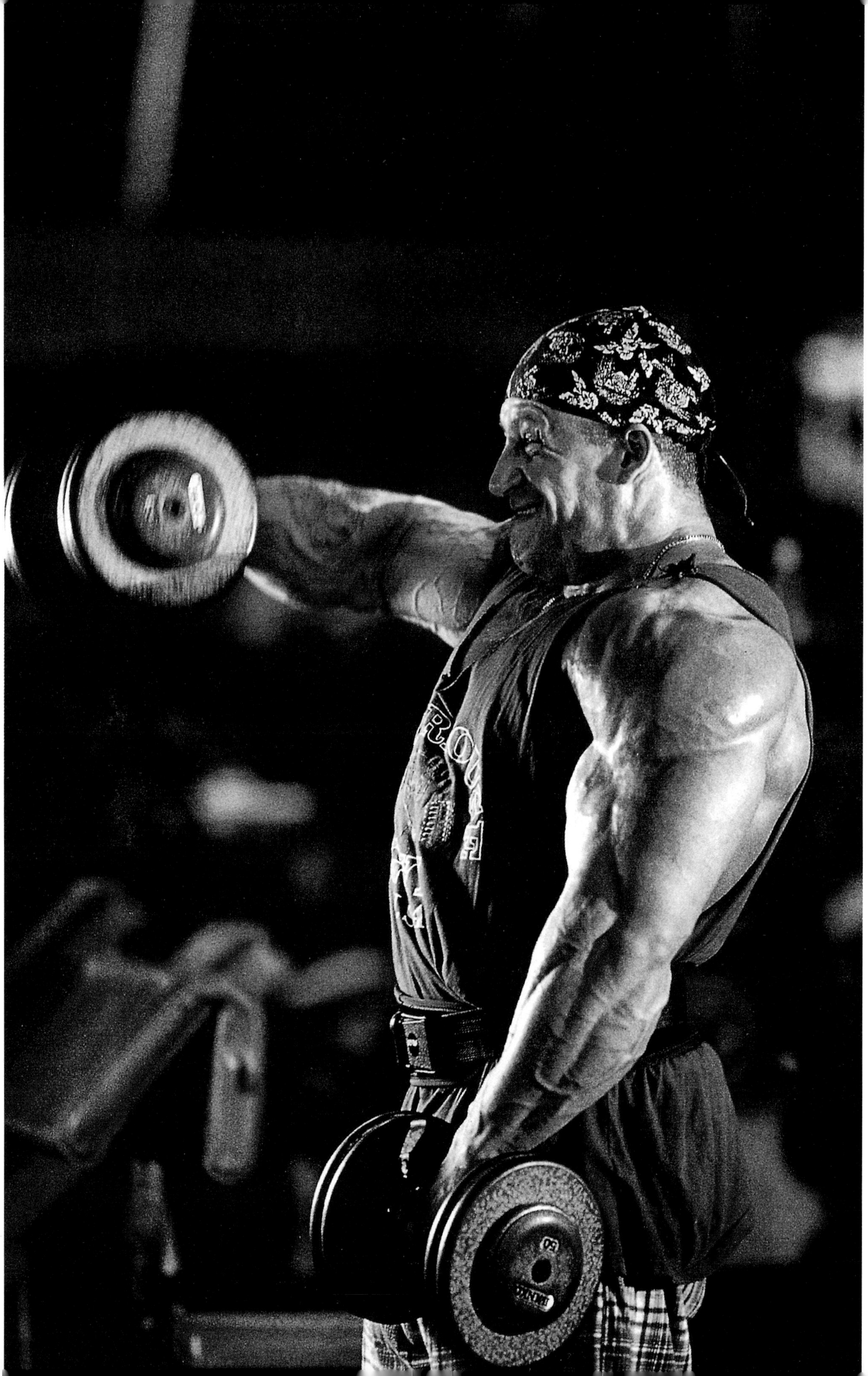

CHAPTER 6

THE BUILDING BLOCKS: Training Principles

The keys to any training program – the elements that give that program its individual character and potency – are the training principles used within that program. So, before getting into the nuts and bolts of my program, it is important to be cognizant of the training principles I use. When I mention any of these principles or techniques later on, you will be aware of what is being discussed.

The principles I use are all to be found among the Weider Training Principles, as first devised by Joe Weider in the 1940s. Joe never claimed to have invented all of these principles, although he did invent some of them. Many of these principles, like forced reps, were being used in those days by weightlifters and bodybuilders without them really being aware what they were doing. What Joe did was identify these techniques, develop them and explain their precise function and use. He then catalogued these techniques into one master list, the Weider Training Principles, and in so doing gave the sport a terminology that brought a new scientific approach to the art of building muscle.

Here's a reprise of the training principles I use. At the conclusion of the discussion of principles, I'll explain the one-main-set system of training I currently follow.

OVERLOAD TRAINING PRINCIPLE

The key to building muscle is to force it to grow by making it respond to a workload it is not used to. For instance, a beginner's arms will be developed only for the everyday tasks of the nonlifter. Once that beginner starts training and does, for example, a set of barbell curls of eight reps with a weight with which he can't do a ninth rep, then he is subjecting his biceps to a workload they have not previously encountered. By way of compensation, the biceps increase in size and get stronger, so that they can handle that ninth rep at a future workout. At that point, the trainee should then add more weight to the bar so that failure again occurs at the eighth rep. Once more, the arms will respond with an increase in size and power so as to accommodate the increased workload. The bottom line is that the overload principle constantly forces muscles to respond to a task they are not accustomed to, so they have to adapt by getting bigger and stronger to handle that load.

A word here on increasing poundages: Don't get impatient and start overloading just for the sake of it. It really doesn't matter what poundage you use as long as it allows you to exert maximum intensity and takes you to true muscular failure within the prescribed rep range while employing textbook lifting style and a full range of motion. I'm often asked what is my best single rep for the bench or squat. I don't know; I've never attempted a single on any lift. I'm a bodybuilder, not a powerlifter. I use weights to sculpt my physique; they are my tools, not my master. The poundages I use are only of interest as a means of monitoring improvements and progress. Don't get drawn into lifting macho poundages, where you may have an impressive weight on the bar but you have to cheat and compromise your lifting technique in order to move it. With that approach, the skeletal frame is placed under more stress than the muscles.

FORCED REPS PRINCIPLE

After the overload principle, forced reps represent my favorite – and thereby most used and effective – training principle. Forced reps, like the majority of training techniques, are a way to extend the set and maintain intensity beyond failure. For instance, for incline barbell presses, I may hit failure at the eighth rep. However, that failure equates to not being able to do another rep with that maximum weight; it doesn't mean I have no reserves of strength left at all. To institute the forced reps principle, once I have reached failure, I will get my partner to gently put his hands under the bar and give me only the assistance necessary to keep the bar moving slowly. With his help, I will complete another two reps; these are called forced reps. By prolonging the set past the normal point of failure, you are upping the ante in stress placed on the muscle fibers and therefore overloading the targeted muscles to the maximum.

REST-PAUSE PRINCIPLE

As with forced reps, the rest-pause principle is used at the end of a set and enables you to extend the set beyond failure. For instance, here's how it's incorporated into a set of machine shoulder presses on which I hit failure around the eighth rep. At that point, I stay seated in the machine and rest for 10 seconds in order to regain some strength. Then, I'll grip the bar again and press out another rep. I'll rest another 10 seconds before doing another – and final – rep. The rest-pause principle is a great strength-builder and is particularly helpful for anyone who doesn't have a training partner and therefore cannot do forced reps.

NEGATIVE REPS (OR REVERSE GRAVITY) PRINCIPLE

This principle is yet another means of extending a set beyond failure. For instance, once I've reached failure on a set of triceps pushdowns, my partner will assist me in raising the stack until my arms are in the fully extended near-lockout position. With my triceps already extremely fatigued, the weight will be heavier than the strength of the triceps can handle. To invoke the reverse gravity principle, I fight and resist the weight as it makes its passage through the negative (lowering) part of the rep, meaning it is lowered as slowly as possible. This action puts maximum stress on the fibers that control the negative part of the rep, and it's a great means of working through a sticking point (i.e., when you're stuck at a certain weight for a certain number of reps and can't seem to increase the load). For safety reasons, it is advised that this principle be used only on machine movements; employing it on free-weight exercises can be clumsy and dangerous.

DESCENDING SETS PRINCIPLE

I use this principle for exercises that, by design, make forced reps less than ideal. One such exercise is the seated dumbbell curl, where I'll drop the dumbbells at the point of failure and pick up a lighter pair and do another two or three reps. Again, this enables me to maintain intensity on the muscle past the point of failure. This is another principle that will prove practical for anyone training alone.

PARTIAL REPS PRINCIPLE

Here's another principle I employ for exercises with which forced reps are impractical. For instance, once I've reached failure while doing side laterals, I'll continue to raise the dumbbells through as high an arc as possible instead of ending the set. Due to my deltoids being fatigued, it could be a three-quarter movement, or it could be a little bit further. The aim is to keep the utmost intensity on the delts by raising the dumbbells as high as strength levels will allow. A typical pattern would be that I'd grind out a couple of three-quarter reps, followed by a couple of half reps and conclude with a quarter-range rep. By that time, my deltoids are absolutely fried.

PRE-EXHAUSTION PRINCIPLE

This principle was initially developed as a means to overcome a sticking point. For example, you may find that your chest is not developing as well as you'd like because your triceps are giving out before your pec muscles on heavy bench presses. This means that the pecs are not being taken to exhaustion: They're not being overloaded and forced to grow. The solution to this problem is to use the pre-exhaustion principle. Pre-exhaust the pec muscles by doing a set of flyes. By virtue of being an isolation exercise, flyes work only the pecs and don't call the triceps into play. After completing the set of flyes, do a set of bench presses. Your pecs will be fatigued but your triceps will be fresh, which will result in your chest muscles giving out before your triceps on the bench presses. In this manner, the pre-exhaustion principle allows you to take your previously undertaxed pecs to failure.

However, I don't use this training principle in the formal sense just explained. I use it when working large bodyparts like thighs and back. When thigh training, for instance, I will do three sets of leg extensions to tire my quads before I move on to leg presses. During my leg-press work, I will use a lighter weight (due to my quads having been pre-exhausted) than would have been the case if I had skipped the leg extensions. The lighter leg presses still allow me to work my already fatigued quads to the max, but I don't have to use superheavy poundages that would put my joints under more pressure than my thigh muscles.

ONE-MAIN-SET TRAINING

The volume-training approach (for example, a program encompassing four exercises per bodypart and five sets per exercise) favored by most bodybuilders never made any sense to me. When I was an amateur, I thought that the volume-training champs were more experienced and perhaps knew something I hadn't yet learned. Once I became a professional and began to mix with other pros, and then observed and talked to some of the champs who use volume training, I discovered that there's not a lot of rhyme or reason for the way they train. It's just accepted that "excess leads to success" and time spent in the gym equates to quicker gains. Question the volume-training champs on why exactly they do the specific amount of work they do, ask them to justify it logically and physiologically, and they won't really be able to tell you.

Eschewing volume training, I concentrated on intensity of effort and never did more than three sets for an exercise, even as a beginner. Over the years, I increased the intensity to the point where I currently do one all-out main set for each exercise. For beginners, I still advise three sets per exercise. It took me nine years (from 1983 to 1992) before I was able to develop the powers of concentration that allowed me to apply myself 100% to one all-out set per exercise. Beginners need more sets in order to perfect lifting technique and to generate the necessary muscle pathways.

Warm up lightly on the first set of each exercise and then work to failure on the subsequent sets. It is not necessary for a beginner to include the extremes of forced or negative reps. I trained for 12 months before I tried a forced rep, and only after two years of workouts did I begin to employ them regularly. For a beginner, going to failure generates enough muscular stress. The "newness" of your body to the rigors of weight-training guarantees the correct muscle-building response will occur. As you progress, you must choose the point at which you can honestly apply the one-main-set system. As already stated, it took me nine years before I felt able to make that move.

A YATES' SET

It must be stressed that the one main set I do takes me to the very limit of my capabilities. For example, my preferred mass builder for chest is the incline bench press. After a couple of warm-up sets with a weight I can easily handle, I load up the bar with the maximum poundage I will use. With that weight, I'll grind out eight or so perfect reps until I reach failure. At that point, my training partner will help me to complete two or three forced reps to failure. Even after that, the set may not be finished. Sometimes, I'll do a couple of negative reps; other times, a couple of reps in rest-pause fashion. You need the aid of a training partner for these techniques. One set with intensity that extreme does the muscle-building job.

For anyone trying this one-set system, if you feel you can attempt a second set, then you couldn't have been pulling out all the stops during the first set. It might be thought that a reduction to a workload of one set per exercise is a radical change, but it wasn't for me because I've never been a believer in volume work. All that I've ever needed to rationalize the one-set approach is what makes sense to me and my physique.

The insurmountable question mark I've always had against doing even as few as three sets per exercise is how to avoid pacing yourself. You're bound to hold back on sets one and two so as to ensure there's enough in the tank for set three. In fact, since I've been doing one set per exercise, I'm continually asking myself how the hell I managed to avoid the pacing dilemma when I was doing two sets per exercise.

I often illustrate the pacing problem by drawing a comparison between a sprinter and a marathon runner. How long can you maintain an all-out sprint before you are forced to jog? The answer is "not very long."

If you do three main sets to failure, it is physiologically impossible to all-out "sprint" on every set. For the sake of argument, even if you were able to maintain 100% effort throughout three sets, the effect would be detrimental anyway. One set with 100% intensity does the job. The message that you need more size and strength has been sent to the muscle. If you hit a nail bang on the head the first time and drive it straight into the wood, what's the point of hitting the nail again? You'll only damage the wood and destroy your own initial efforts. It's my contention that to send a second or third message via a high-intensity set confuses the muscle-building process. You'll end up spending more time recovering from your workouts than growing from them.

With the building blocks of my training philosophy firmly in place and acting as the foundation, let's move on to constructing the rest of the bodybuilding edifice.

Forced Reps

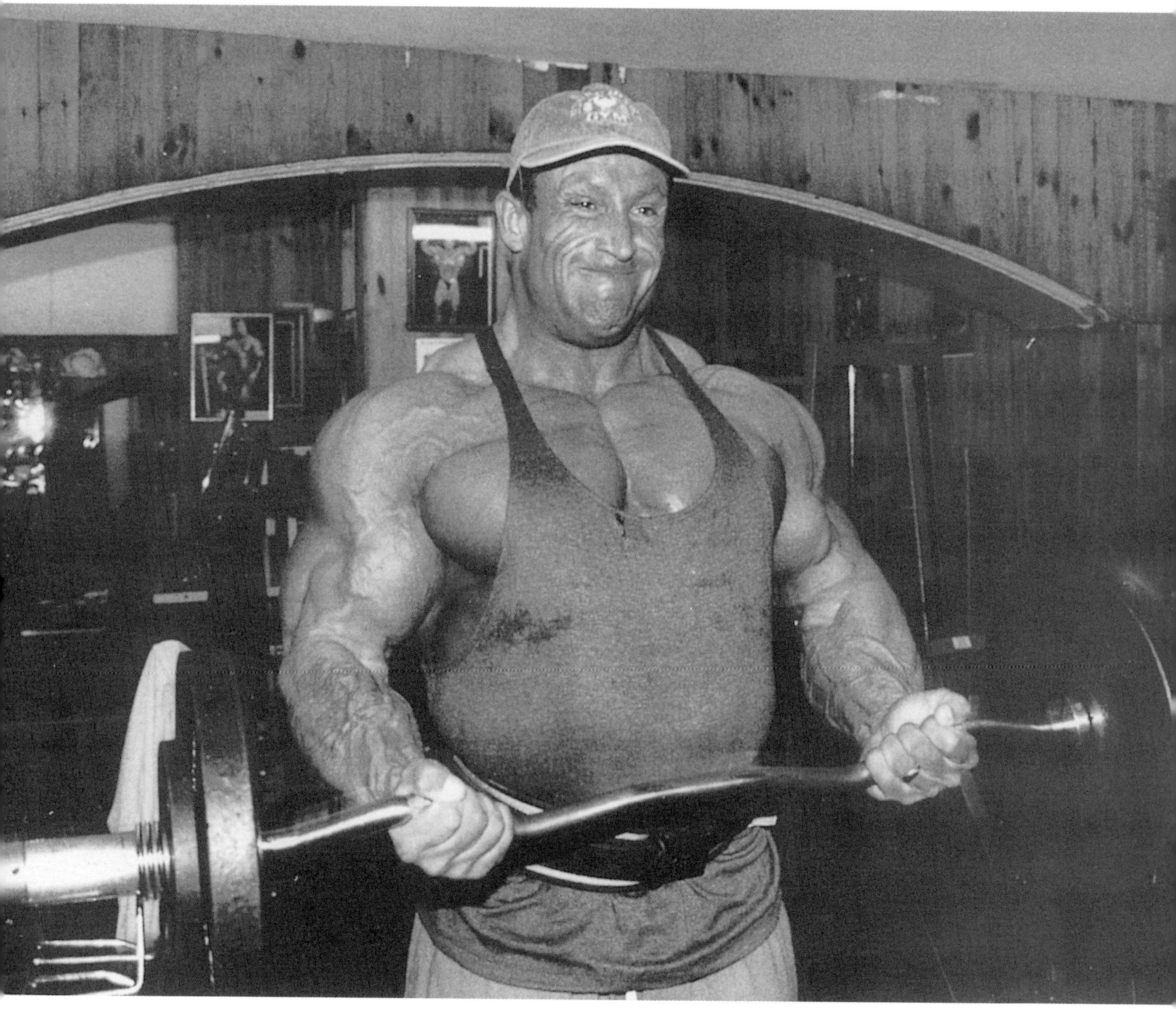

CHAPTER 7

THE FULL MONTY:
My Complete Training Program

I've always had a reputation for being unorthodox, so, true to that persona, I'm going to start the workout program content of this book at the end of the training story. Namely, I will map out the training program I currently use, the one with which I won the 1995, '96 and '97 Olympia titles. This training program is the culmination of the 12 years of research, analysis and on-the-gym-floor trial-and-error that preceded its 1995 inception.

I'm not suggesting that you jump straight into following me rep for rep. My strategy is that an explanation of this program will reveal the fundamentals that represent my training philosophy. From that base, we will backtrack, and I'll explain in Chapters Eight and Nine how you can go from rank beginner status to the advanced level, with the goal being that you will arrive at the ideal training program for you. In Chapters Ten through Sixteen, I will break down the program bodypart by bodypart and give a full explanation of exercises, exercise technique and all matters specific to each bodypart. The net result is that all will be clear – the full monty will be revealed.

ON THE WINGS OF 1994

The year 1994 was a watershed year for me. In the run-up to that year's Olympia, I sustained three serious injuries: rotator-cuff damage, a quad tear and a biceps tear – all on the left side of my body. By the time of the contest, the quad tear had healed, but I took my third Olympia title with my biceps and rotator-cuff problems having decimated my precontest training.

The prognosis on the biceps tear was that as the muscle had not detached from the bone, it would not require surgery and was best left to heal on its own. As for my damaged shoulder, I underwent arthroscopic surgery for it on October 24, 1994. I thought recovery from the surgery would take five or six weeks, so with my biceps healing fast, I thought I would be back in full training by the middle of January '95.

I was too optimistic. For the six months following my surgery, my left shoulder still felt weak and out of whack with my right side, and I was unable to handle the poundages I wanted to. It wasn't until April of 1995 that I felt able to fire on all cylinders.

Still, I was confident the time remaining would be enough for me to peak at my all-time best on Olympia day (September 9), because the revisions to my training (introduced as a reaction to my triple injuries) had already, despite the restricted time allowed, borne muscular fruit. The revisions were threefold, and I'm detailing them because I think that, although I resorted to them because of injury, you would be well-advised to adopt these techniques from day one.

THE TRIPLE WHAMMY

First, I reduced the poundages I was using and upped the reps slightly. Broadly speaking, this meant using poundages with which I would hit failure in the eight-to-ten-rep range, whereas, previously, I used poundages with which failure would occur between reps six and eight.

The second change had to do with the execution of movements. Prior to my injuries, I would resist during the negative part of each rep and then explode out of the midpoint into the positive part of each rep.

Instead of that "resist-explode" sequence, I evolved a style wherein instead of exploding into the positive part of each rep, I moved the weight in a slower and more precise fashion. For instance, when doing incline presses, I now remove the bar from the rack and lower it slowly to my upper chest, before pushing the weight back to the starting point with an evenly powered and controlled (nonexplosive) movement. This style made for a fuller and more deliberate muscular contraction, because throughout the completion of each rep (both the negative and positive phases), the muscular overload was constant. By comparison, the practice of exploding into the positive phase means that the stress on the pec muscles is uneven. The explosiveness generated is such that, after the initial thrust, momentum takes over to a certain extent and lessens the muscular stress during the middle and latter parts of the movement.

The third aspect of fine-tuning involved the use of more machines in my workouts. I've always been a free-weights advocate, but in pursuit of a more precise execution of movement tied into the goal of lessening the risk of injury, I accepted that machines offered a greater margin for safety than is the case with free weights.

I didn't consider these changes a radical departure from the training philosophy I had followed since I began bodybuilding in 1983. It wasn't like I had suddenly switched to doing five sets of 20 reps per exercise. It was just a fine-tuning of the beliefs that had taken me to the Mr. Olympia title. The constants were all still there: I was still completing one main set to failure and beyond; my training frequency was unaltered; and the reps were still pretty low. The focus was still on achieving the most intense muscular contraction in the shortest possible time, and then getting the hell out of the gym in order to allow sufficient time for recuperation.

The instigation of these three modifications (slightly higher reps and lower poundages, more deliberate style of execution, and greater emphasis on machine work) meant that I still applied the maximum amount of muscular stress possible, while at the same time substantially reducing (and hopefully eliminating) the injury risk factor.

ROWING TO A DIFFERENT STROKE

My revamped style of barbell rowing makes for a good illustration of how I modified my training in 1995 in comparison to previous years.

I tore my left biceps in July 1994, while barbell rowing with 405 pounds. Up to the point of sustaining that injury, my method of executing barbell rows was as follows: Using a curl grip, I would grasp the bar and, keeping my arms straight, I would lift the bar off the ground while setting my upper torso to an angle of 70 degrees. I would then arch my back and power the weight up until it made contact with my midriff. From that point, I would release the weight to the starting position and then immediately power it back up again. In that nonstop style, I'd complete five or six good reps. Once failure was reached, I'd grind out a three-quarter rep and finish with a half rep. You can't do forced reps while barbell rowing.

My revised barbell-rowing m.o. requires that I grasp the bar with an overhand grip: This lessens the stress on my previously injured left biceps. My present maximum is 375 pounds and, after assuming a position where my upper body leans forward at an angle of 70 degrees, I pull the weight up to my midriff. At that point, I hold the weight for a second or so in order to stimulate the full peak-contraction effect, and then I release the bar very slowly to the starting position. Unlike the previously explained method of execution (where motion is continuous), I pause at the starting position before repeating the procedure. Failure occurs around the eighth to tenth rep, from which point I'll complete a three-quarter rep before finishing with a half rep.

Even though I've never been a slouch in the back department, this more precise style of execution helped me to improve my back for my Olympia appearances from 1995 onward.

MY OWN WORST ENEMY?

As stated in Chapter Two, I formulated my training philosophy using Mike Mentzer's Heavy Duty high-intensity principles as a base. The proposition that my injuries prove that high-intensity training is self-defeating is a load of rubbish. How much do you want to take your foot off the intensity pedal? Hey, if you stay at home and don't train at all, you won't get injured. When you're pushing your body to the limit, there's always some risk involved. Over the years, I could have trained less intensely to avoid injury, but that less-than-100% commitment wouldn't have taken me to the Olympia title.

My injury problems stemmed from the fact that my mind tried to take my body to places it wasn't strong enough to go. Bodybuilding is a mental as well as a physical journey, and my body had to give my mind the warning light that it was time to shift the focus. The injuries were the warning light.

The way I rationalize my injuries is to say that after over a decade of consistent training, my ability to generate power had become a danger to my skeletal structure. To draw an automobile analogy, it's like I started out driving a beat-up Volkswagen and finally ended up at the wheel of a Formula One racing car. Thrash the Volkswagen as much as you like and (because of the limited power available) you'll come to no real harm, but with the Formula One model, one minor miscalculation could mean you're staring disaster in the face.

DAMAGE CONTROL

The training revisions I made had been generated in reaction to an injury crisis; the effect on my physique didn't reflect a mood of making the best of a bad job. Quite the contrary, my more precise approach to working out led to physique improvements. That's why I'm advocating you employ these aspects to your training with immediate effect.

If you review my physique of 1993, you'll note that it was hard and I was in very good condition. However, compared to my physique at the 1995, '96 and '97 Olympias, the '93 version seems a little raw: "unfinished" is how I'd sum it up. From '93 to '95, hardness, size and condition are comparable, but the model from 1995 onward has much more detail, especially in the smaller muscle groups. For instance, there was more detail in my teres major, hams, pecs and delts.

To me, the lesson was clear. By submitting my physique to a more precise and controlled execution of movement, I was maintaining the intensity, as well as achieving a fuller and more comprehensive muscular contraction within each individual muscle group. I am sure that this more precise form of exercising the muscles stimulated growth in finer areas and muscle fibers that previously had not been stimulated.

I arrived at this precise method of lifting in part because of the injuries, but it led to an improvement in my physique. That's why I'm strongly advising – OK, I'm telling you – that you should lift with the same style as I do now.

Throughout my career, the setbacks I've had always seem to happen for a reason: There always seems to be an underlying lesson to be learned. The 1994 triple-injury debacle was really the wake-up call that what had served me well for more than a decade was now in need of modification. Not only was the fine-tuning beneficial to my physiological health, it improved my physique – gave it a more "finished" look. Like I say, everything happens for a reason.

GETTING WITH THE PROGRAM

The training split and program shown in this chapter represents my training schedule from 1995 onward. It is a four-way split, wherein I train four days out of seven. Apart from abs, I do one all-out set for each exercise. The chart lists warm-up sets. For most main sets, I do two or three forced reps and sometimes employ negative, rest-pause, or partial reps. For some bodyparts (as will be explained in individual chapters) I do a form of pre-exhaust and with some exercises I institute descending sets.

This program has proved to be my most productive. In the next chapter, we'll start the process of moving toward formulating your own most productive training program.

A PORTRAIT OF DORIAN YATES 51

THE ULTIMATE ROUTINE: DORIAN'S MR. OLYMPIA-WINNING PROGRAM

TRAINING SPLIT
Day one: Delts, traps, triceps, abs
Day two: Back, rear delts
Day three: Rest
Day four: Chest, biceps, abs
Day five: Rest
Day six: Quads, hams, calves
Day seven: Rest

WORKOUT ONE

Warm-up: Ten minutes on stationary bike, followed by gentle stretching of all muscle groups to be trained.

BODYPART	EXERCISE	SETS	REPS	POUNDAGE
DELTS	Smith machine presses	1*	15	120
		1*	12	240
		1	8-10	340
	Seated laterals	1*	12	2 x 50
		1	8-10	2 x 70
	One-arm cable laterals	1*	20	35
		1	8-10	70
TRAPS	Dumbbell shrugs	1*	12	2 x 140
		1	10-12	2 x 185
TRICEPS	Triceps pushdowns	1*	15	80
		1*	12	130
		1	8-10	180
	Lying barbell extensions (with an EZ-curl bar)	1*	12	100
		1	8-10	140
	One-arm pushdowns or	1	8-10	70
	One-arm Nautilus extensions	1	8-10	full stack
ABS	Forward crunches	3	20-25	
	Reverse crunches	3	12-15	

A PORTRAIT OF DORIAN YATES   53

WORKOUT TWO

Warm-up: Ten minutes on stationary bike, followed by gentle stretching of all muscle groups to be trained.

BODYPART	EXERCISE	SETS	REPS	POUNDAGE
BACK	Hammer Strength machine pulldowns	1*	15	135
		1*	12	220
		1	8-10	285
	or (alternated each workout)			
	Nautilus pullovers	1*	15	220
		1*	12	320
		1	8-10	440
	Barbell rows	1*	12	285
		1	8-10	375
	One-arm Hammer Strength rows	1	8-10	245
	Cable rows (overhand grip)	1	8-10	full stack
REAR DELTS	Rear-delt Hammer Strength machine			
		1	8-10	2 x 55
	Bent-over dumbbell raises	1	8-10	2 x 95
LOWER BACK	Hyperextensions	1	10-12	40
	Deadlifts	1*	8	310 *
		1	8	405

WORKOUT THREE

Warm-up: Ten minutes on stationary bike, followed by gentle stretching of all muscle groups to be trained.

BODYPART	EXERCISE	SETS	REPS	POUNDAGE
CHEST	Incline barbell presses	1*	12	135
		1*	10	220
		1*	8	310
		1	8	425
	Hammer Strength seated bench presses	1*	10	220
		1	6-8	350
	Incline dumbbell flyes	1*	10	2 x 75
		1	8	2 x 110
	Cable crossovers	1	10-12	2 x 90
BICEPS	Incline dumbbell curls	1*	10	2 x 50 *
		1	6-8	2 x 70
	EZ-curl barbell curls	1*	10	100
		1	6-8	140
	Nautilus curls	1	6-8	120
ABS	Forward crunches	3	20-25	
	Reverse crunches	3	12-15	

54 A PORTRAIT OF DORIAN YATES

WORKOUT FOUR

Warm-up: Ten minutes on stationary bike, followed by gentle stretching of all muscle groups to be trained.

BODYPART	EXERCISE	SETS	REPS	POUNDAGE
QUADS	Leg extensions	1*	15	130
		1*	12	200
		1	10-12	270
	Leg presses	1*	12	770
		1*	12	1045
		1	10-12	1265
	Hack squats	1*	12	440
		1	8-10	660
HAMSTRINGS	Lying leg curls	1*	8-10	130
		1	8-10	180
	Stiff-leg deadlifts	1	10	350
	Single leg curls	1	8-10	50
CALVES	Standing calf raises	1*	10-12	900
		1	10-12	1300
	Seated calf raises	1	10-12	250

* Warm-up sets

A PORTRAIT OF DORIAN YATES

CHAPTER 8

STARTING OUT: Complete Training and Diet Program for Beginners

A regular occurrence at my seminar appearances is beginners telling me they are in awe of me as Mr. Olympia, and that my physique, to them, is unattainable, so why bother training at all. I always tell them, "You and I are not that much different. If I can fulfill my physical potential, you can fulfill yours." What I mean is that not everyone can be Mr. Olympia, but everybody, with planning and application, can be the best they can be. If you become the best bodybuilder you can be, then your achievement is every bit as worthy as my winning six Sandow statues.

I've been told by many bodybuilders – including professionals – that they feel they wasted their first two years in the sport by jumping from one program to another, overtraining and generally going up blind alleys. The first two years are crucial. If you make substantial progress, it stokes your bodybuilding appetite for life. On the other hand, early days that are filled with frustration are often a precursor to dropping out of the sport altogether. Whether by good fortune or design, I feel I didn't waste my first two years. If I can do it, you can, too!

IN THE BEGINNING

To be called a beginner is not an insult. Every Mr. Olympia was once a beginner. In my estimation, the beginner's phase lasts for about two years. You won't be surprised to learn that the beginner's bodybuilding program I am promoting is almost a duplication of the one I used for my first two years as a bodybuilder.

I started bodybuilding in 1983 as a means to do something positive with my life; it was a challenge to see how good I could be. I was lucky in some ways that when I started training, I didn't have direct access to a top-class bodybuilder from whom I could seek advice. I say "lucky," because I had to learn what worked for Dorian Yates right from day one. There wasn't the opportunity to be sucked into the slipstream of the beliefs of someone else who – a beginner might assume – "knew better."

I read everything I could concerning bodybuilding and nutrition. (This is a practice I still follow today, much to my wife Debbie's annoyance. She says our house is like a library.) I mentally weighed everything I read, questioning whether or not it would work for me.

During those first two years, I'd assess certain exercises, techniques and nutritional tips, then select what I thought would be right for me. Not everything I tried worked, but I gained the confidence and the instinct to drop something as soon as I realized it wasn't for me. I wouldn't try to convince myself that because a certain champion used a specific method, it must work for me.

If I have one message for bodybuilders of all levels, it would be that you are the best judge in the world of how your body responds, or doesn't respond, to the components of your bodybuilding program. Listen to the signals from your body. Don't ignore them.

BEGINNERS' INDUCTION

During the research I did in the weeks prior to my first workout, I found myself greatly influenced by the writings of Mike Mentzer. I decided that the optimum way to muscle growth was to follow a training schedule of a high-intensity complexion. But before rushing into a high-intensity program, I had to acquaint myself with the nuts and bolts of bodybuilding.

For the first six weeks of my bodybuilding career, I trained my whole body three times a week on nonconsecutive days, which allowed adequate recuperation time. The routine (see Table One) involved one basic exercise for each bodypart and represented my induction course into bodybuilding. I advocate that you follow the same induction course. It is an invaluable means of getting used to the gym – the loading and unloading of bars and machines. It will teach you the rudimentary techniques of lifting and make you cognizant of the range of motion for each exercise. The program allowed me to experience how my muscles felt and reacted during and after a training session, and it will do the same for you.

In order to develop correct technique, each rep must be performed strictly. My rep target was just inside my strength capabilities. There was no goal of training to failure: I was simply trying to find the right groove for each exercise. You must do the same.

I'd planned to utilize this "breaking-in" program for a maximum of eight weeks or a minimum of four, and I urge you to follow a similar time frame. After six weeks, I felt I'd completed the necessary apprenticeship and decided it was time to move on to a split routine.

THE SPLIT ROUTINE

An example of a split routine is a system wherein the body is divided into halves, with each half being trained during alternate workouts. This means you can devote more time to each bodypart while also allowing more time for recuperation.

Initially, the split routine I devised (see Table Two) called for me to train four times a week: on Monday, Tuesday, Thursday and Friday. After a week and a half of adhering to this schedule, I felt tired and stressed out, as if my nervous system was out of whack. I was obviously doing too much and

A PORTRAIT OF DORIAN YATES 59

60 **A PORTRAIT OF DORIAN YATES**

my body was sending me a distress signal.

The schedule was revised so that I trained every other day, but even that proved too ambitious for my body's reserves. Eventually, I settled on training three days a week, which meant that over a 14-day period, I worked each half of my body three times, as follows.

Week One

Monday ....Workout One
Tuesday ....Rest
Wednesday ....Workout Two
Thursday ....Rest
Friday ....Rest
Saturday ....Workout One
Sunday ....Rest

Week Two

Monday ....Workout Two
Tuesday ....Rest
Wednesday.........Rest
Thursday ....Workout One
Friday ....Rest
Saturday............Workout Two
Sunday ....Rest

The premise that a training program should be in sync with a seven-day cycle was almost sacred back in 1983, but I had no qualms about breaking that tradition. Human physiology ticks to a 24-hour clock, not a seven-day calendar, and I was doing what was best for Dorian Yates.

Within this split routine, I did three exercises for large bodyparts and two exercises for the smaller ones. The exception was thighs (a large bodypart), which I limited to two exercises: barbell squats and hack squats. At that stage of my development, I felt those were the only two exercises I needed for thighs – I did an extra set of barbell squats by way of compensation. Like my induction course, my split routine relied mainly on basic movements, as they generate the most overall growth.

I rested between sets only as much as I needed, and I didn't socialize during rest periods. I was very businesslike: My job was to get in and out of the gym as quickly as feasible, and then go home and grow! Another factor that illustrated that I had stepped up a gear from my "breaking-in" schedule was that I started to compile a training log. This was an invaluable reference in determining what worked for me and what didn't. (For more on the benefits of keeping a training diary, see Chapter Eighteen.)

After a year on this schedule, I started to include forced reps. I would choose one basic exercise for each bodypart and at the end of the last set of that exercise, I would do one or two forced reps.

THINK BEFORE YOU LIFT

From day one of starting bodybuilding, I was very aware of approaching a workout in the correct frame of mind. I don't think anyone can get good results by just walking into a gym and starting a workout without any thought of what he or she is trying to achieve. Always take time to psych yourself up prior to a workout and lock your mental energies into what is required. Get clear in your own mind what you perceive as the goals for that particular workout, and convince yourself of how hard you will have to work in order to achieve them. You may have the ideal training program, state-of-the-art supplementation and a well-planned diet, but without willpower and a positive attitude, your progress will be inhibited.

When I began split-routine training, I weighed 180 pounds, and I kept on it for two years right through to my first novice contest in 1985, when I weighed 210 pounds. In fact, I didn't abandon this program until after I won the British heavyweight division in October of 1986. I can give my first split routine no higher recommendation than if I had to do it all over again, I would follow the same program.

BEGINNERS' DIET

I was working shifts in a factory during my first four years of training while trying to support Debbie and our son Lewis (who arrived in 1984), so money for bodybuilding foods and supplements was scarce. I drew up a plan of eating six small meals a day. For bodybuilding purposes, it is better to feed the body consistently throughout the day rather than overload it with three large meals. (My typical daily menu for that time is detailed in Table Three.)

The only supplements I was able to afford were a multivitamin/mineral pack, which I took during breakfast (most supplements are better absorbed if taken with food), and a milk/egg protein-shake powder. Even if money had not been a problem, I think (as someone in his first two years of training) I would have added only amino acids to my supplementation program.

When I commenced split-routine training in 1983, my total daily caloric intake averaged 3,500, which rose to 4,000 by 1985. Those calories were divided into the ratio of 30% protein, 55% carbohydrate and 15% fat.

Protein is the prime ingredient in the muscle-building process. Without an adequate daily intake of protein, you won't build muscle tissue. On a daily basis, you should consume 1 1/4 grams of protein for each pound of bodyweight. Carbohydrate is the fuel that supplies energy for your workouts. An intake of fat is also necessary to keep the physiological system functioning normally, as well as contributing to other factors such as healthy skin and hair. I allowed myself more fat in those days (I currently limit fat to 10%), because I was in an important phase of growth and wasn't obsessed with being permanently cut to the bone.

Using the dietary parameters described above and in Chapter Seventeen as a guide will help to maximize your muscle growth. However, don't become preoccupied by consuming excess calories in pursuit of that growth. You can't force-feed muscle growth, but you can force-feed the accumulation of fatty deposits. I grew on 3,500 calories a day, so I would advise that you be satisfied with making gradual bodyweight gains of good quality – between one and two pounds a month – rather than spectacular increases in bodyweight, which will be mostly in the form of fat.

If you start to gain fatty tissue, cut back on your calories. If you begin to feel tired and stressed, increase your carb intake slightly.

TABLE ONE

INDUCTION PROGRAM

Warm-up: Ten minutes on stationary bike, followed by gentle stretching of all muscle groups to be trained.

BODYPART	EXERCISE	SETS	REPS
Thighs	Barbell squats	3	10
Hamstrings	Leg curls	3	10
Chest	Bench presses	3	10
Back	Barbell rows	3	10
Shoulders	Behind-the-neck presses	3	10
Biceps	Barbell curls	3	10
Triceps	Lying triceps extensions	3	10
Abs	Crunches	3	20
Calves	Standing calf raises	3	10

DURATION: approximately 50 minutes

TIPS

* Concentrate on using strict style for each rep.
* Use a weight with which 10 reps is just possible, rather than going to failure.
* Rest between each set until you are fully capable of completing the next set. The time period should fall between 60 and 90 seconds.
* Listen to what your body is telling you in regard to the suitability of each exercise.

TABLE TWO

SPLIT ROUTINE: 1983-1985

WORKOUT ONE

Warm-up: Ten minutes on stationary bike, followed by gentle stretching of all muscle groups to be trained.

BODYPART	EXERCISE	SETS	REPS
CHEST	Bench presses	3	8
	Incline presses	3	8
	Incline flyes	2	8-10
BACK	Chins or pulldowns	3	8
	Barbell rows	3	8
	Deadlifts	3	8
DELTS	Behind-the-neck presses	3	8
	Side laterals	2	8
	Bent laterals	2	8
ABS	Crunches	3	to failure
	Hanging leg raises	3	to failure

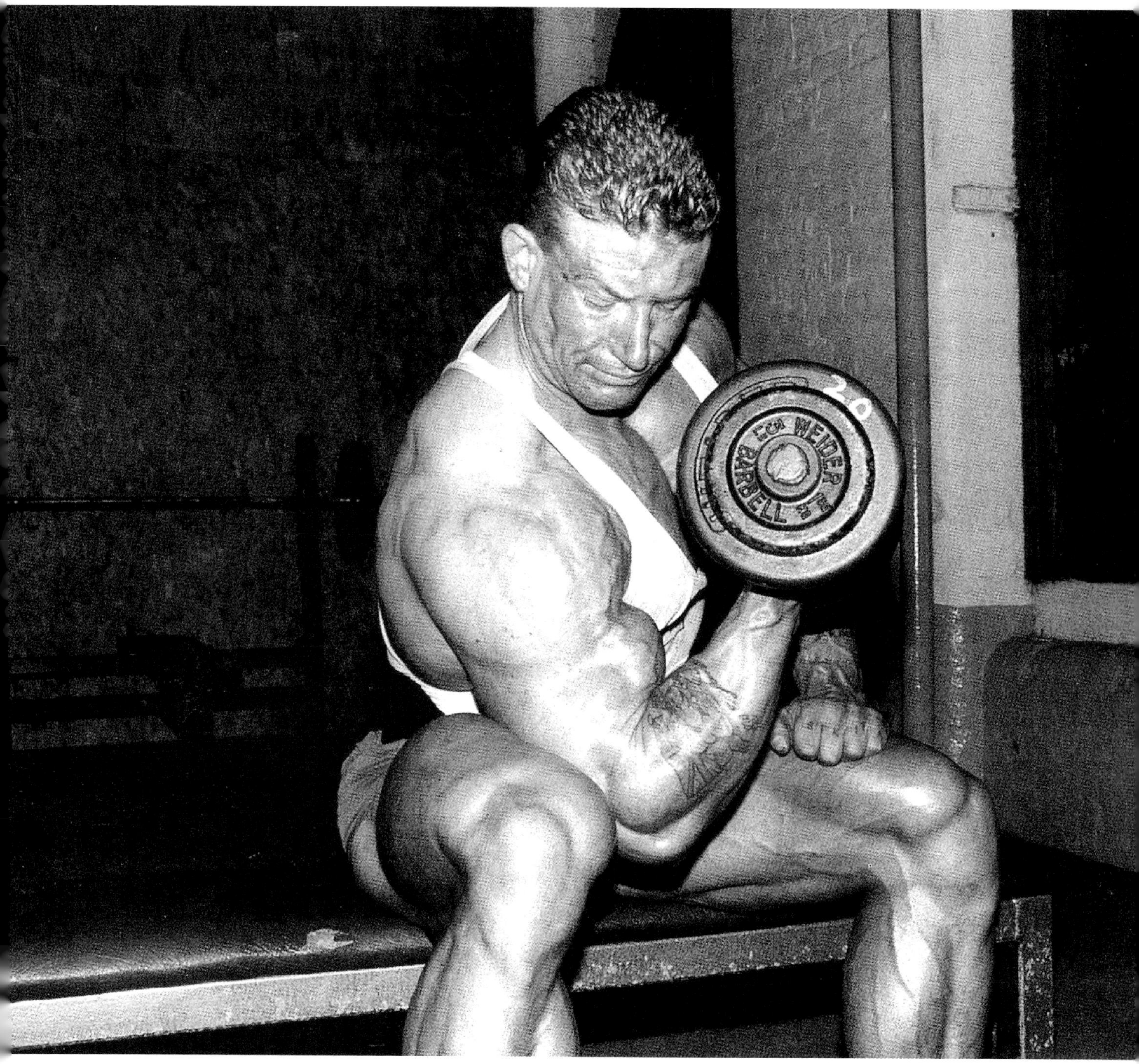
WEIDER
BARBELL
20

WORKOUT TWO

Warm-up: Ten minutes on stationary bike, followed by gentle stretching of all muscle groups to be trained.

BODYPART	EXERCISE	SETS	REPS
THIGHS	Barbell squats	4	8
	Hack squats	3	8
HAMSTRINGS	Leg curls	3	8
CALVES	Standing calf raises	3	8
BICEPS	Barbell curls	3	8
	One-arm preacher curls	2	8
TRICEPS	Triceps pushdowns	3	8
	Lying triceps extensions	2	8

DURATION: approximately 60 minutes for each workout

TIPS

* Aim for textbook execution on every exercise.
* The first set of each bodypart should be relatively light (to warm up), with the following sets taken to failure.
* When the eighth rep no longer represents failure, add weight accordingly.
* Don't employ forced reps until you've been following this schedule for 12 months.

TABLE THREE

TYPICAL DAILY MENU: 1983-1985

Breakfast	five whole eggs, scrambled
	two slices of whole-wheat toast
	bowl of oatmeal (with skim milk)
	multivitamin/mineral pack
Midmorning	serving of milk-egg protein shake
	(mixed with skim milk)
	banana
Lunch	chicken breast or tuna
	baked potato
	two cups of assorted vegetables
Midafternoon	serving of milk-egg protein shake (mixed with skim milk)
	orange
Evening meal	eight-ounce steak
	baked potato or rice
two cups of vegetables	
Supper	bowl of oatmeal
	4 egg whites
	1 egg yolk

A PORTRAIT OF DORIAN YATES

CHAPTER 9

THE ADVANCED LEVEL: Complete Training and Diet program

The passage from beginner/intermediate to advanced status should not be dramatic. The upgrade should represent a smooth transition, one that doesn't hinder or jar your progress. The transformation should be made only when you're ready for it. If you're ready, you won't have a problem. If you do have a problem, you're not ready and should stay with the intermediate training program for a little while longer. Here's how I made the change.

In the previous chapter, I explained the training and dietary program I followed from 1983 to 1985. In fact, I kept the training part of the program intact for another year, but I fine-tuned my diet and added other elements that I'll detail in due course.

After winning my first novice contest in July 1985, I set my sights on the 1986 British Championships, which were to be held in October of that year in London. For that contest, I followed the same workout program I had used since 1983.

I didn't revise my workout schedule because I believe in the maxim "If it ain't broke, don't fix it." The program had served me well, and I knew there was still an appreciable amount of muscle mileage left in it. My proportions were fairly good, so I didn't have any particular bodyparts designated as priorities. It was a matter of getting bigger, harder and denser, while keeping those proportions in balance.

In a training sense, the thing that did change was that I was getting stronger and lifting heavier poundages. More on that later.

The major change I made following my contest debut concerned diet. I didn't alter the carb/protein/fat split or range of foods, but I did substantially increase the number of calories. My offseason high had previously been 4,000 calories, which led to a bodyweight high of 235 pounds (my 1985 contest weight was 210 pounds). In 1986, I consumed as many as 5,000 calories a day during the offseason and hit a bodyweight high of 255 pounds.

During that period, my main goal was to increase size and power; I wasn't nearly as meticulous with my offseason diet as I am now. I didn't weigh each portion: It was more a matter of guestimating. Twelve weeks before the '86 British Championships, I began my contest countdown and cut back to an average of 2,500 calories a day. I also introduced another element I had never used before: a cardiovascular conditioning program!

CARDIO-WORK

I devised an aerobics schedule in which I completed three 30-minute sessions of stationary cycling each week. These sessions were completed in the evenings on days I wasn't weight training. I now place a greater importance on aerobics, and I realize that my original regimen wasn't as effective as it could have been. I've come to learn that aerobic exercise is much more productive when done first thing in the morning, prior to eating. At that point, the body is depleted of glycogen and is more amenable to burning fat as a source of fuel.

At the 1986 British Championships, I won the heavyweight division, but failed to win the overall decision. Looking back, I can see I overdid my size-gaining policy in the offseason. From a bodyweight high of 255 pounds, I came down to 214 and probably lost some muscle size in the process. Although I gained more quality and density, I was only four pounds heavier than at my contest debut in July 1985.

SPLITTING THE SPLIT

In the aftermath of the 1986 British Championships, I knew it was time to reevaluate my two-way training split. Losing the overall wasn't the cause. It was a case of realizing that, as I became stronger, the effort of working three bodyparts in one training session was becoming harder and more draining. So I devised a three-way split in which I worked two major bodyparts per training session instead of three (see Table One).

Within this split, each bodypart was worked three times over a 14-day period as follows.

Week One
Monday ....Workout One
Tuesday ....Workout Two
Wednesday ....Rest
Thursday.................Workout Three
Friday ....Rest
Saturday ....Workout One
Sunday ....Workout Two

Week Two
Monday ....Rest
Tuesday ....Workout Three

A PORTRAIT OF DORIAN YATES

Wednesday ....Rest
Thursday ....Workout One
Friday...................Workout Two
Saturday...............Rest
Sunday ....Workout Three

With the two-way split, I had been training three days per week; the three-way split called for me to work out four times a week. However, I was working fewer bodyparts during a training session and I also reduced the main set requirement from three sets to two sets. With my greater strength levels, I knew I could get the job done in two sets rather than three. Overall, the changes meant I was in the gym for a shorter period at each training session and still ensuring sufficient recuperation time.

A LEANING FOR SIZE

In previous offseasons, my primary aim was to build size. But in the offseason that preceded the 1988 British Championships, I committed myself to staying as lean as possible.

As with all bodyweight changes, the key ingredient was diet. A big influence on me at that time was Rich Gaspari (Mr. Olympia runner-up, 1986-88). He was really strict about monitoring his caloric intake, which culminated in his highly shredded condition. In keeping with my escalating passion to go all the way, I started to stringently calculate my own caloric intake.

My calories were still split in the ratio of 30% protein, 55% carbohydrate and 15% fat, but I made a subtle change in emphasis. I was now much more concerned about obtaining a better spread of correct nutrients rather than a preoccupation with eating an appropriate amount of calories to boost my bodyweight.

I began to weigh and measure everything I ate, no longer content to use loose measurements, such as a "bowlful" or "spoonful." I became much more fastidious. Before, I'd never worried about having a snack from McDonald's from time to time, but now that kind of treat became a rarity.

Offseason, I took in as many as 5,000 calories daily. (For a specific breakdown, see Table Two.) I was eating just enough to allow me to slowly add good bodyweight instead of bulking up for the sake of it. I used fruits as a carbohydrate source much more than I do currently. Fruits contain simple carbs (mainly fructose), and I now understand that complex carbs, such as potatoes and other vegetables, are a much more efficient source of energy (due to having slower-release properties than simple carbs) for a bodybuilder.

THE STRENGTH CURVE

As stated earlier, a main reason for changing my workout routine after the 1986 British Championships was that my strength levels were overtaking my recovery abilities. I'm a great believer in the premise that stronger muscles become bigger muscles. As you progress, you definitely have to consistently increase the poundages you use while still adhering to good form. Apart from visual and measured proof of muscle growth, strength is one of the main indices of progress. Increased poundages and physique advancement go hand in hand. If poundages weren't important, then I'd still be squatting with the same 150 pounds I used when I started bodybuilding.

In 1985, after two years of training, my maximum squat routine featured 380 pounds for 10 reps. By early 1988, even though I was by then pre-exhausting my thighs with leg extensions, I was handling

465 pounds for 10 reps. The fact that my thigh size and musculature increased in tandem with my strength was no coincidence. I smile when I hear other bodybuilders say that they use the same poundages year after year.

With the intensified strategy I adopted following my hip surgery in 1987, I was much harder in the offseason than I had ever been previously. Carrying a much lower percentage of bodyfat, I had much less weight to lose when I began my 12-week precontest countdown for the 1988 British Championships. For the '86 championships, I started from a bodyweight high of 255 pounds and, on a precontest diet of 2,500 daily calories, dropped 41 pounds and competed at 214 pounds. For the '88 event, I started from a high of 250 pounds and, on a precontest diet of 3,000 daily calories, dropped 24 pounds and came in at 226 pounds. With both diet and physique, there was now less of a gap between my offseason and precontest periods.

On October 19, 1988, I took the British heavyweight and overall titles. That made me a professional with new fields to conquer.

The routines outlined in the previous chapter and this one had added 46 pounds of muscle to my frame in five years and taken me from complete novice to pro status. Is it any wonder that I strongly advise you to construct your early training days around these programs? After all, they served as the launching pad for a pro career that would eventually bring me six Mr. Olympia titles.

TABLE ONE – THREE-WAY SPLIT

WORKOUT ONE

Warm-up: Ten minutes on stationary bike, followed by gentle stretching of all muscle groups to be trained.

BODYPART	EXERCISE	SETS	REPS
Chest	Bench presses	3	6-8
	Incline barbell presses	2	6-8
	Dumbbell flyes	2	6-8
Biceps	Barbell curls	3	6-8
	One-arm preacher curls	2	6-8
Triceps	Triceps pushdowns	3	6-8
	Lying extensions	2	6-8
Abs	Hanging leg raises	2	15-20
	Crunches (with weight)	2	15-20

TIPS

* The first set of the first exercise for each bodypart (except abs) is a warm-up for that muscle group. Therefore, you will do two all-out sets of each exercise.
* On each all-out set, I went to failure and concluded with two forced reps.

WORKOUT TWO

Warm-up: Ten minutes on stationary bike, followed by gentle stretching of all muscle groups to be trained.

BODYPART	EXERCISE	SETS	REPS
Thighs	Leg extensions	3	12-15
	Barbell squats	2	12-15
	Leg presses	2	12-15
Hamstrings	Leg curls	2	8-12
Calves	Standing calf raises	2	8-10

TIPS

* Leg extensions were introduced as a technique to pre-exhaust the thighs prior to heavy squatting.
* I suggest higher reps for thighs, because they respond better to higher reps.

WORKOUT THREE

Warm-up: Ten minutes on stationary bike, followed by gentle stretching of all muscle groups to be trained.

BODYPART	EXERCISE	SETS	REPS
Back	Weighted chins	2	6-8
	Barbell rows	3	6-8
	Cable pulley rows	2	6-8
Delts	Bent laterals	2	6-8
	Barbell shrugs	2	6-8
	Behind-the-neck presses	3	6-8
	Side laterals	2	6-8

TIPS

* Before commencing chins, I warmed up with two light sets of pulldowns.
* Do barbell rows to failure; you can't do forced reps safely with this movement.
* After going to failure on shrugs, I did three or four partial reps.
* The first set of behind-the-neck presses acted as a warm-up.

TABLE TWO

A TYPICAL DAILY OFFSEASON MENU: 1986-1988

Breakfast	six egg whites with two yolks
	150 grams of oats
	50 grams of raisins
	three slices of whole-wheat toast
	1/4 pint of skim milk
	orange
	multivitamin/mineral pack
	five peptide-bond amino-acid tablets

Midmorning	pint of skim milk blended with two scoops of milk/egg protein powder
	orange
Lunch	seven ounces of tuna
	100 grams of pasta
	two oranges
	carbohydrate drink
	five peptide-bond amino-acid tablets
Midafternoon	**Workout**
Post-training	pint of skim milk blended with two scoops of milk/egg protein powder
	three bananas
	two protein bars
Evening Meal	eight ounces of chicken or steak
	300 grams of baked potato
	200 grams of mixed vegetables
	pineapple
	five peptide-bond amino-acid tablets
Supper	five egg whites and one yolk
	slice of whole-wheat toast
	25 grams of raisins
	five peptide-bond amino-acid tablets

TOTAL: 5,000 calories

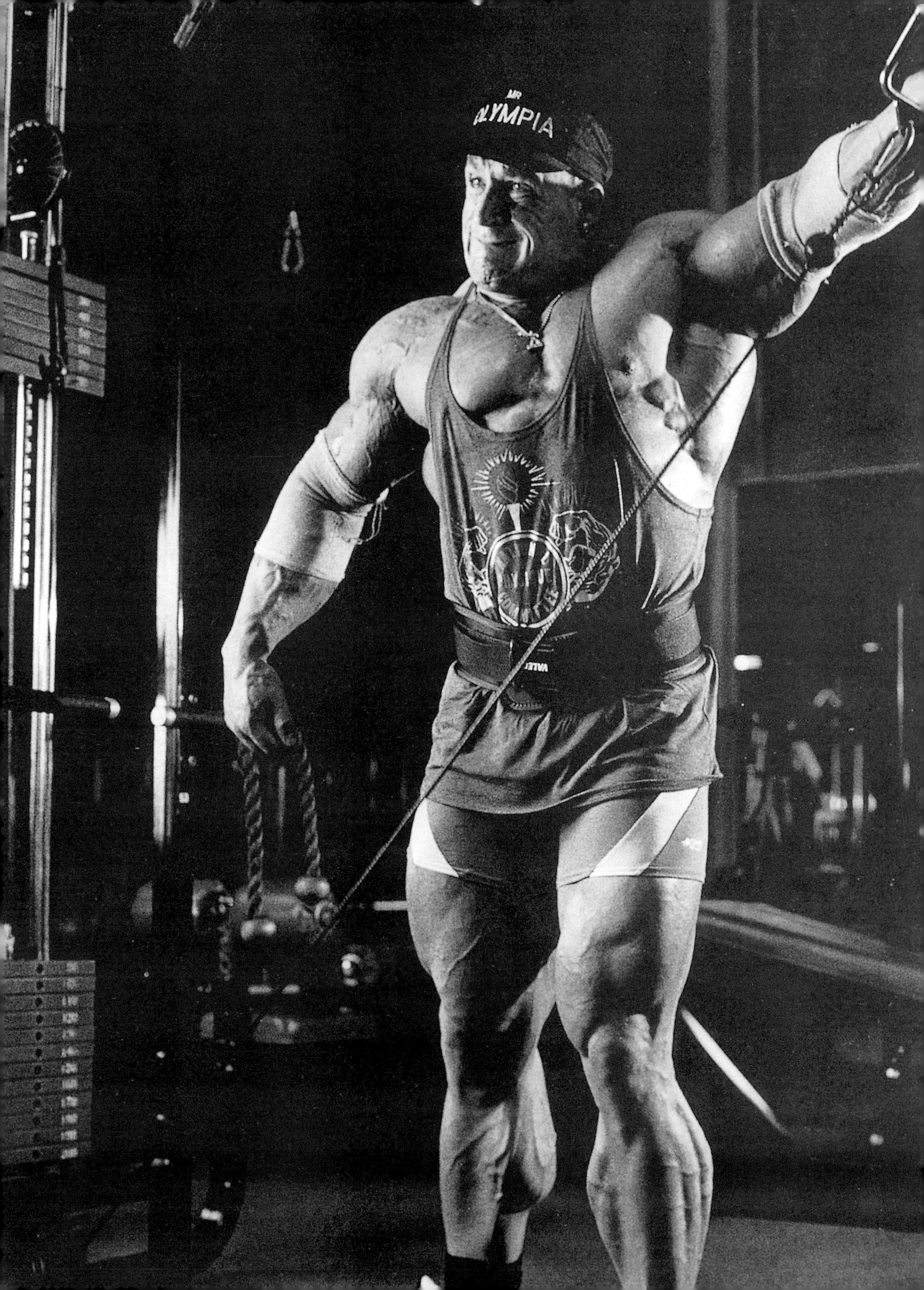
MR
OLYMPIA

CHAPTER 10

ON GIANT SHOULDERS: Deltoids and Traps

While it's commonly accepted in mainstream circles that clothes make the man, in the more exposed environs of competitive bodybuilding, a truer maxim is that shoulders make the bodybuilder! First impressions are all-important, and no aspect of a physique has more immediate impact than a set of wide and thickly developed delts. At the opening bell of a bodybuilding contest, nothing packs a wallop like a pair of knockout delts.

When rating a physique during a bodybuilding competition, eyes are first drawn to shoulder width. Broad shoulders are essential in sculpting a symmetrical physique and they are also the prime element in displaying a V-taper. Width (courtesy of the side delts) is crucial, but when a physique is viewed from the side, the front and rear delts must be equally well-developed in order to show thickness in harmony with width. All too often, a bodybuilder spoils his first impression of width by turning to the side and disappearing.

To achieve optimal shoulder development, you must realize that you are not exercising a single muscle but a complex muscle group, comprised of three distinct muscle heads: the anterior head (front delt), the medial head (side delt) and the posterior head (rear delt).

In order to achieve muscular accord between the three heads, a balanced program of exercise must be followed in which the front, side and rear deltoids are developed in tandem with each other. Such a coordinated schedule ensures that each individual head receives the appropriate amount of stimulation, with no sector of the deltoid triumvirate growing out of proportion or lagging behind.

A PORTRAIT OF DORIAN YATES

For me, this balancing act requires constant fine-tuning, because my front delts have always responded quickly, while my side and rear delts have proved to be a shade more stubborn. In fact, I don't include rear-delt work in my shoulder routine. My rear delts are so intrinsic a part of the jigsaw that represents total back development that it's better to incorporate them into my back-training schedule.

JOINT DECISIONS

One negative aspect of shoulder training is the ever-present specter of injury. Along with the lower back, shoulder joints are probably the most susceptible sites for bodybuilding injuries – I've got the doctors' appointments to prove it. I sustained my series of shoulder injuries despite training in a safe style; if you use poor exercise form on delt work or overtrain them, then you're really asking for trouble.

A proper warming-up program is essential for all bodyparts, but this is particularly true for injury-prone shoulder joints. I warm up with a light series of side, front and bent lateral raises. One set of each with 20 reps gets the blood flowing and makes the area as muscularly flexible as possible. I also stretch the delts back and forth while holding a broomstick overhead.

PRESS FOR MASS

My first shoulder exercise is a compound pressing movement. Such movements work all three deltoid heads and help pack on mass around the whole shoulder girdle. In my earlier days, I used to favor behind-the-neck presses. I still think they are great for beginners and intermediates. The problem with this exercise is that, as you increase your strength levels and use heavier poundages, you begin to place unacceptable stress on the shoulder joints while doing what is an unnatural movement. All the barbell has to do is drift a little too far behind you, and you can strain the joints.

After abandoning behind-the-neck presses, I used dumbbell presses, but, here again, my strength began to outstrip the boundaries of safety. I reached the point of doing my main set with 150-pound dumbbells, and their sheer physical dimensions made them clumsy and difficult to control as I reached failure. So I again went looking for a compound pressing movement that represented a safer option.

Seated Smith machine presses were the answer. Since they follow a guided groove, I can pile on as much weight as I want, which means I can actually press more poundage to arms' length than with dumbbells. This movement also enabled me to feel the exercise more, because I'm able to concentrate more on pushing the weights than on controlling their pathway. When you're using 150-pound dumbbells, as I was, you expend a lot of energy just balancing them, but if you have 340 pounds on a guided machine, you can concentrate solely on using your deltoid muscles.

I position myself at the Smith machine with the bar resting at the fully extended overhead level. I grasp the bar with a grip slightly wider than shoulder width, release it from its resting position and bring it down to shoulder level. From that point, I press upward until just short of lockout position and repeat the rep. This nonlockout procedure means that the delts are under constant pressure throughout the duration of the set. If you lock out, the triceps support the weight and the delts get a rest. During my main set, my training partner will keep his hands cupped just under the bar and, when I reach failure, he will help me grind out a couple of forced reps. For variety, I will sometimes forgo the forced reps and do a couple of rest-pause reps.

LATERAL THINKING

My next exercise is seated dumbbell side laterals. This is the prime movement for bringing out the cap to the side deltoids. By doing them in a seated position, I make the exercise stricter by minimizing body movement. I'll do one warm-up set of 12 reps with a pair of 50-pound dumbbells. I then begin my main set, aiming for eight to ten reps with a pair of 70-pounders. I sit on the end of a bench and start the set with the dumbbells tucked under my legs. I then power into the movement, forcing my arms straight out to the sides, with my palms facing the floor and my elbows slightly bent. I raise the dumbbells to shoulder level (going above parallel means the traps would take over) before letting them descend in a controlled fashion to the starting position. Allowing the dumbbells to simply drop would mean losing the muscular benefits from the negative part of this movement.

When failure is reached, my partner helps me complete two or three forced reps. To keep the intensity going, I will then stand up and cheat out a couple of more reps before I finish the set with as many partial reps as I can achieve. Basically, I fry the side delts by just keeping on going until I can't move the dumbbells at all.

With dumbbell side laterals, I'll sometimes use the triple-drop technique. This entails going to failure with 75-pounders, whereupon I immediately grab a pair of 50-pounders and go to failure with them before finally picking up a pair of 35-pounders and repping out to failure with those.

THE CABLE GUY

My final deltoid exercise is cable side laterals, performed with one arm at a time. It might seem like I'm duplicating the dumbbell work, but cables and dumbbells have distinct characteristics. With dumbbells, a feeling of extreme muscular tension doesn't occur until nearly halfway through the upward swing. With cables, however, severe muscular tension is constant throughout the movement, particularly when you stand a little bit away from the pulley machine and let your arm be pulled across your body. With cable side laterals affording the opportunity of working one arm at a time, this exercise has its concentration advantages also.

After a warm-up set of 20 light reps, my main set of cable side laterals will call for a weight with which failure will set in around eight to ten reps. When failure is reached, my partner assists me in completing two or three forced reps.

When forced reps are no longer possible, I'll do four or five negative reps. This is achieved by having my partner lift the stack to the midpoint position (where the pulley handle is parallel with the shoulder), from where I resist as the weight slowly descends.

TRAPPED

Optimum trapezius development is fundamental to giving the shoulder region a finished and complete look. Traps also lend a certain ruggedness to a physique: a most muscular without big traps shooting through is like Abbott without Costello. The other advantage to good trap development is that they act as stabilizing muscles for the deltoids during pressing movements and lateral raises. Strong traps make all shoulder movements that much safer and more productive.

Up until 1995, I used to train traps with heavy barbell or machine shrugs. I had built up to using 650 pounds and never considered doing dumbbell shrugs, assuming that if I could pull 650 pounds with a barbell, equivalent dumbbells would have to weigh 325 pounds each, and there's no such thing.

Besides, I was getting good results from using a barbell, so it was virtually inconceivable that anything else could work better.

Then, in April 1995, I incurred a forearm strain; nothing serious, but enough of a nuisance to prevent me from applying full intensity with a barbell. Out of curiosity, I decided to try dumbbells, which I thought might give the injury a chance to heal. I did not expect great results, but, to my surprise, I got them. I quickly realized that dumbbells give me a much different and fuller range of motion, followed by a squeeze that can't be duplicated when using a barbell. As a result, my traps improved considerably, not only at the top where they tie in to the delts and neck but also the lower traps where they extend to tie in to the teres major, rhomboids and lats. The latter aspect greatly adds to my overall back thickness.

For shrugs, I do one warm-up set followed by one heavy set to failure, continuing with half or three-quarter partial reps for a burn until I can do no more. Repetitions are 10 to 12. For the main sets, I start with a 185-pound dumbbell at each side, not in front. While many bodybuilders roll their shoulders forward when they shrug, I bring mine straight up, then roll them back and squeeze my shoulder blades together so I can really feel it in my middle and lower traps. Formerly, I tried to use the same rolling movement with a barbell, but I now realize that it was too restrictive. With a barbell in front of your body, you can't bring your hands back to fully contract your scapulae.

At the end of each repetition, I let my shoulders relax and hang loose in order to get another full range of motion up and back. I try not to worry too much about keeping my arms rigidly straight – that's unnatural. If they bend a little bit, it doesn't really matter, as long as I'm getting a full movement with my shoulders and traps.

I also find that keeping my head down, with my chin on my chest, helps me get a better range of motion. With the barbell, I always thought I was getting a full range, but I obviously wasn't. I urge everyone to go for the more complete range of motion for shrugs that dumbbells allow.

WINNING FORM

Strict form is essential when doing shoulder work, which means you shouldn't be obsessed with handling heavy poundages. Although I lift relatively heavy, I've progressed slowly over 15 years to my current strength levels, always maintaining strict form. Some guys sacrifice form for poundage, forgetting that each deltoid head is a small muscle located near a delicate joint structure. The shoulder joint doesn't offer a sound mechanical base on which to bounce prodigious poundages, so using overly heavy weights with sloppy form is not only an impediment to muscular gains, it can also be a prelude to injury.

Treat your shoulder joints with respect and care. Follow the guidelines contained within this chapter and bodybuilding longevity will be yours. To paraphrase a well-known saying: "Old shoulders never die, they just grow and grow!"

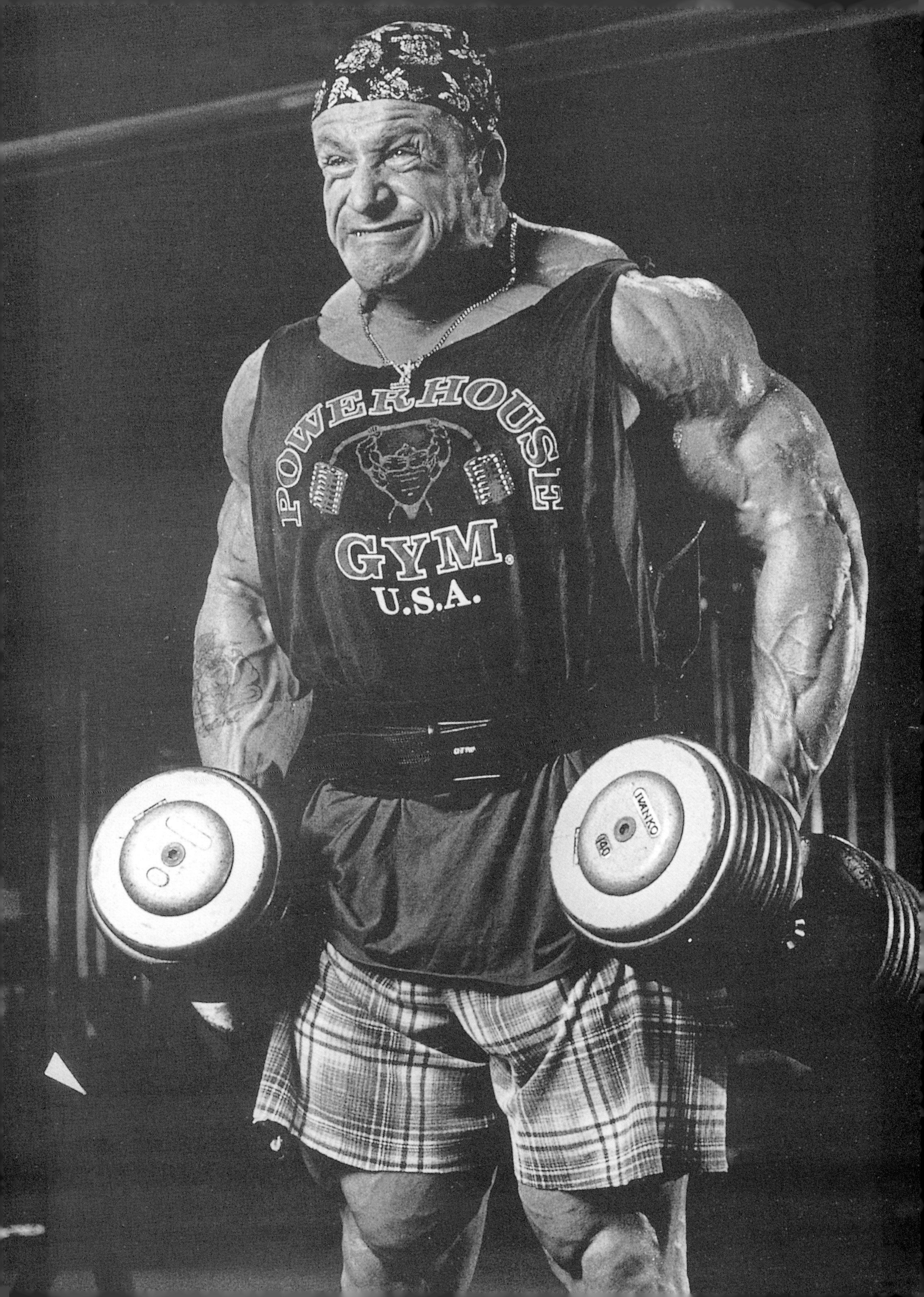
POWERHOUSE
GYM
U.S.A.

DELT-AND-TRAP WORKOUT

	EXERCISE	SETS	REPS	POUNDS
DELTS	Smith machine presses	1*	15	120
		1*	12	240
		1	8-10	340
	Seated laterals	1*	12	2 x 50
		1	8-10	2 x 70
	One-arm cable laterals	1*	20	35
		1	8-10	70
TRAPS	Dumbbell shrugs	1*	12	2 x 140
		1	10-12	2 x 185

* Warm-up sets

A PORTRAIT OF DORIAN YATES

82   **A PORTRAIT OF DORIAN YATES**

CHAPTER 11

TRI, TRI, AND TRI AGAIN: Triceps

A triceps workout shouldn't entail a lot of volume. This is because the triceps are used when any pressing or pushing exercise is performed. During a bench press, for instance, the triceps have to work nearly as hard as your pecs. The same applies to shoulder exercises, such as overhead presses. Because the triceps are stimulated during shoulder work, I choose to train them after delts.

Another reason to keep the volume low during triceps training is due to it being a relatively small muscle (though not as small as biceps) and because the tendon of the triceps is somewhat fragile. I know that from experience. My triceps injury in 1997 was a result of microtears that accumulated over time. I've always taken care while training this bodypart. I didn't experience the tear because of a single trauma, I simply didn't give the smaller pains I felt in my elbow area enough time to completely heal. Keep that in mind if you notice discomfort in your triceps tendon area, but if you feel good, go all out for this bodypart.

With triceps, I favor machine and cable work. I'm not a big fan of behind-the-neck free-weight work for shoulders or triceps. These are unnatural types of movements that can contribute to injury in the shoulder and triceps areas. Some guys are dogmatic about free weights, claiming that using them is the only way to bodybuild. I disagree. Your muscles don't know if you're lifting cable plates, dumbbells or a Spice Girl. Your muscle fibers only know that they're being forced to work.

Triceps are vitally important for both strength gains and physique presentation. If you want to continue adding inches to your chest, you've got to make gains in triceps size and power to

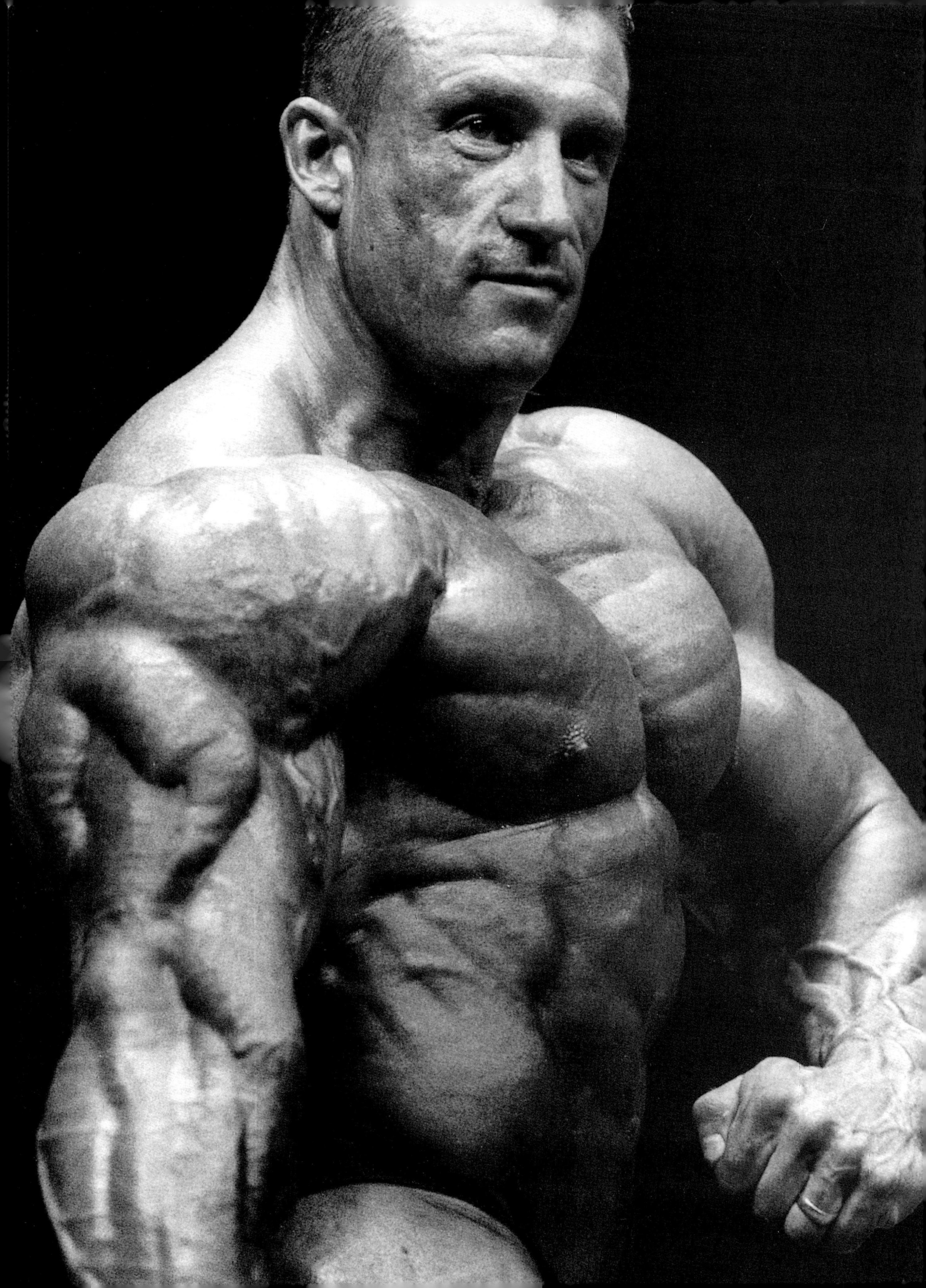

accommodate the increased poundages you will use for pec exercises. The same applies with those shoulder exercises in which you want to increase your pushing power. As regards competition, complete triceps development (which means a hanging mass effect with horseshoe detail) is essential for not only the side-triceps pose but when doing double-biceps (front and rear) and side-chest shots. That's why you always have to pay attention to triceps, working them with just the right amount of weight, sets and reps.

I try not to overcomplicate matters, so the meat of my triceps routine is made up by two exercises, cable pushdowns and lying triceps extensions, both of which are overall mass builders for the triceps. My third triceps exercise serves as the period to the exclamation mark.

PUSH FOR MASS

I usually employ a V-shaped bar for pushdowns. I find that this bar forces my grip into the perfect hand spacing. In the past, I've used a straight bar, but I find the V-bar superior. As regards rope pushdowns, I've never done those. I think the kneeling rope pushdown, in particular, is unproductive. It's not easy to generate optimum power while awkwardly positioned in that way.

With all bodyparts, I believe in a thorough warm-up. Even though my triceps have already been worked by my previous shoulder movements, I first do a light warm-up set of pushdowns for 15 reps, followed by another set with moderate weight for 12 reps. Only then do I move on to my main set.

The pushdown is a direct straightforward movement that's very difficult to bungle. Keeping your elbows at your sides and moving only your lower arms, simply push down to lockout, then release the pressure slowly until the bar is just below your nipples. At that point, don't let up on the tension as you begin the pushdown movement again. Throughout the set, try to keep the bar close to your body; don't lean forward as you push down, as this takes some of the stress off the triceps. For my third set, I go heavy, hitting failure between eight and ten reps. When failure is reached, I grunt out a couple of forced reps to finish the job.

EXTENSIONS

My second exercise is the lying triceps extension with an EZ-curl bar. I use the EZ-curl bar instead of a straight bar because it helps me to place my wrists in a more comfortable position and it alleviates stress on my shoulder and elbow joints.

Start this movement by lying along the length of a bench and holding the bar overhead. I do this exercise a little different than many bodybuilders do. The orthodox way to proceed is to lower the bar to the forehead and then press it back until the bar is directly over the face. I lower the bar to a point just beyond my head. I then press the bar back up at an angle that puts the bar -- when the arms are almost straight -- directly above the starting position: i.e., a point just beyond my head. It may appear that you are pushing the weight backward at an angle. It's not really a backward motion; it's actually a straight up motion, but it can feel like you're pushing backward. I don't lock out at the top position. This maintains constant stress on the triceps.

I feel that the modified arc of motion that I employ keeps the stress more directly on the meat of the triceps than is the case when following the orthodox plane of movement. The latter style also puts extra pressure on the elbow and shoulder joints.

I do a set with moderate weight before getting to my main set. I'll aim for eight to ten reps in the working set, and I'll finish off with two forced reps when I reach failure.

One final word on extensions: This is a very strict movement, so perfect your technique with a light weight before you incorporate it into your heavy-duty weight regimen. You always need someone to spot for you on this exercise: They're not called skull crushers for nothing.

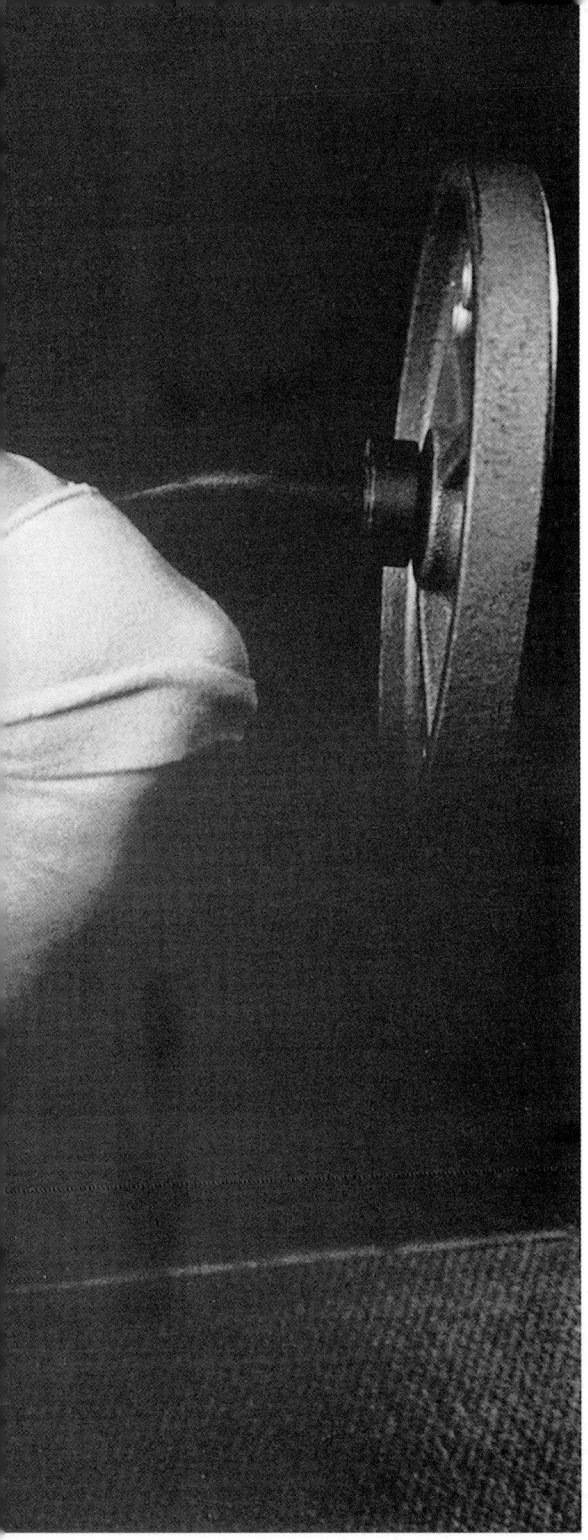

UNILATERAL ARMS

For my final triceps movement, I'll switch gears a bit and do one set of a unilateral movement. The two choices I favor are cable pushdowns with a reverse grip or one-arm extensions on a Nautilus machine. After doing extremely heavy two-handed exercises, I want to get a different stress to finish off the muscles. Unilateral movements offer the facility of being able to maintain continuous tension, and they allow me to get a deep burn into each triceps. I do only one set with each arm for my last triceps exercise, but it's an intense set.

Reverse-grip pushdowns provide continuous tension in a unique way. No other exercise mimics this action, which is like pulling down a window shade, and I do pull all the way down to lockout. I do a full set with one arm before switching to the other arm. It's the same for the Nautilus triceps machine. Once failure is reached, I throw in a couple of forced reps to complete the job. That last killer rep, even with your other arm assisting, can boost growth like no other rep.

Don't overdo the volume on triceps work and pay attention to even small pains. Know the difference between healthy muscle soreness and connective-tissue stresses. If you feel confident, go balls to the walls, because your triceps need to be strong if you're going to make consistent overall gains.

TRICEPS WORKOUT

EXERCISE	SETS	REPS	POUNDS
Triceps pushdowns	1*	15	80
	1*	12	130
	1	8-10	180
Lying EZ-curl barbell extensions	1*	12	100
	1	8-10	140
One-arm reverse-grip pushdowns	1	8-10	70
or			
One-arm Nautilus extensions	1	8-10	full stack

* Warm-up set.

A PORTRAIT OF DORIAN YATES

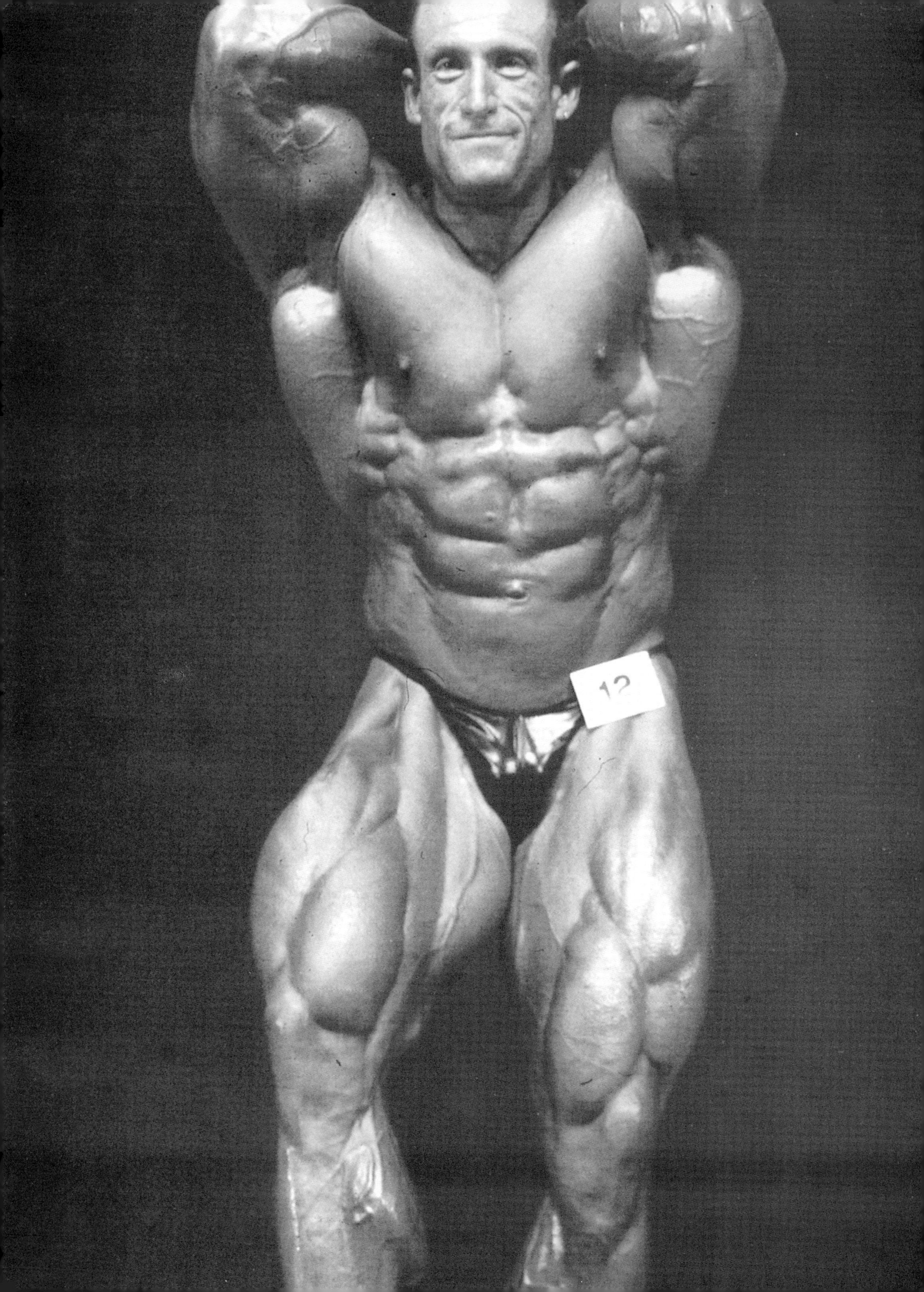
12

CHAPTER 12

THE MIDDLE GROUND: Abdominals

Contrary to popular thinking, the abdominals are more than "show" muscles. You'll never be able to build a thick, strong back if your abs aren't also strong. A blight of 20th century man is back pain, which can often be linked to weak abs. The martial-arts world puts great credence on ab strength, believing it is the center of power. For instance, try to do any movement – or even try to shout – and you'll find that you first brace your abs. The abs also act as stabilizer muscles in many compound exercises such as squats, curls and presses. The fact that the abs are called into play during so many exercises is a major reason why they don't have to be worked as often as you may think.

Another important aspect to understand about abdominal training is that these muscles are at the mercy of genetics and diet more than most. You can't create a six-pack if you have a four-pack. Once you diet down and see what you have, that's it. Whatever genetics have dealt you, that's what you have to work with. The trick is to make your abdominals as dramatic as possible.

GUT REACTION

Even nonbodybuilders crave a good midsection, hence all the silly little contraptions out there designed to spot train. Spot training is basically a misguided concept. These strange ab devices promise an easy way to a washboard stomach. The manufacturers assure results if you rock away in a flimsy plastic jigger. The only result you are assured to get is to be jiggered out of your money.

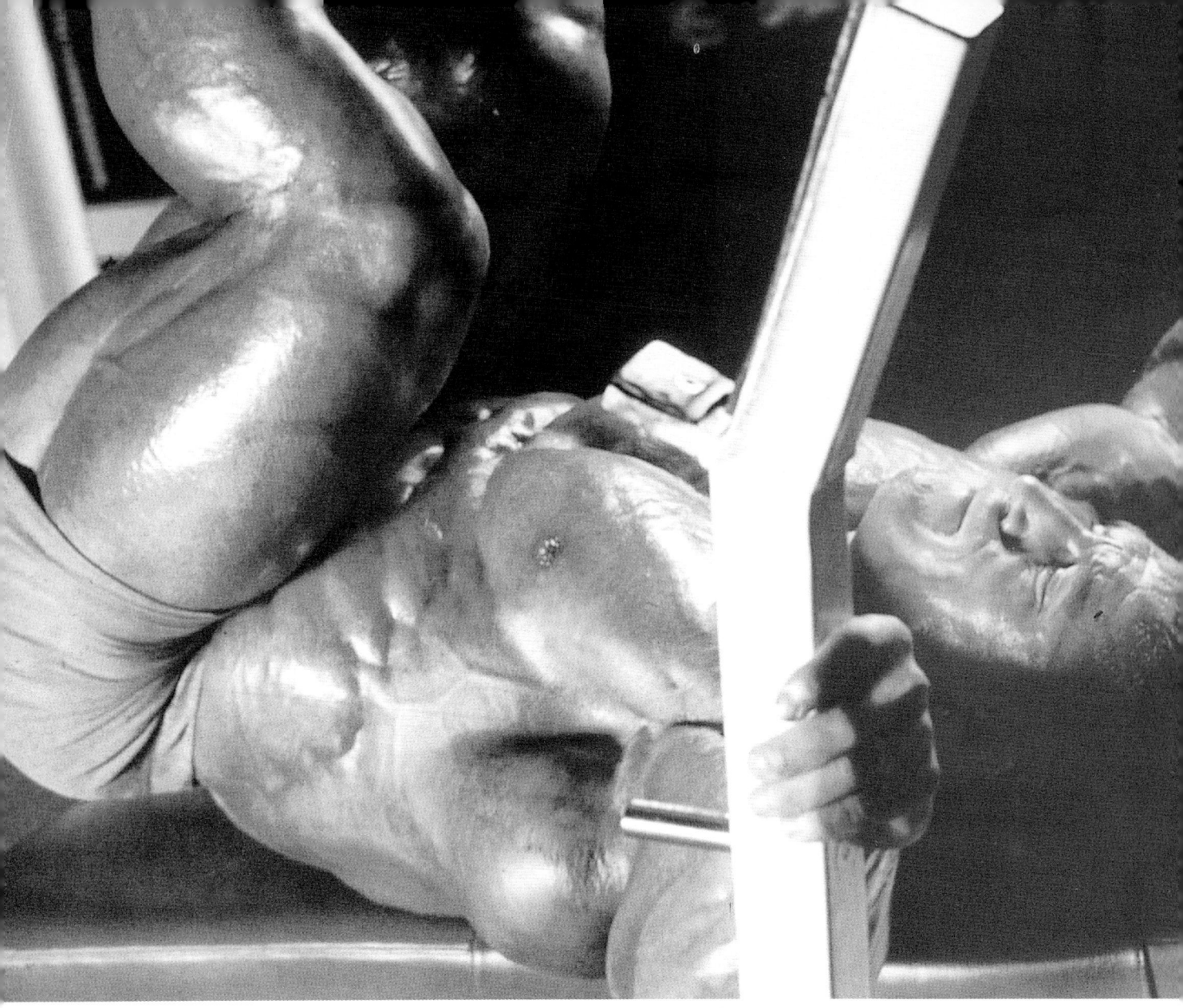

Reverse Crunch

Working abs is really a simple process. I do only two exercises: forward and reverse crunches. I think crunches are the most efficient movements for abs, providing direct stimulus. I feel full-fledged sit-ups and leg raises are no-nos for a couple of reasons. First, they are powered more by the hip flexors than the abs. Second, they spread out the stress too much and put too much pressure on the lumbar region. Either way, sit-ups and leg raises shortchange the full ab complex.

I work abs once a week during the offseason, twice a week precontest. I used to train them more often at the beginning of my career, when I was trying to build thickness. You may see guys with 45-pound plates clutched to their chests while they do crunches. You probably don't have to go to that extreme, but if abs are a weak area for you, go ahead and provide extra stress. Once you hit the advanced stage of development, cut back on your more intense ab work and develop a program that maintains the condition you've developed in that region.

I was lucky to have good abs before I began training. You may already have good musculature in your midsection and not know it, if you have not dieted down sufficiently. Always keep that in mind before you become frustrated with not seeing your abs. It probably isn't a training defect, but it may be a diet malfunction.

THE CRUNCH

The actual journey of a perfect crunch is only a matter of a few inches. It's a short contraction, as you bring your pubic bone toward your chest. Both forward and reverse crunches work the whole ab region, but the forward version emphasizes the upper abs a little more while reverse crunches give extra stimulus to the lower abs.

For forward crunches, I lay on my back on the ground and drape my legs over a bench. While stabilized on the floor, I put my hands behind my head. Moving only my head and upper back off the floor, I raise my rib cage toward my legs until I feel a contraction in my abs. At that point, I hold the position and squeeze for a count of three before returning to the starting position. As I said, it's a short movement, and I do three sets of 20-25 reps.

Reverse crunches are a bit trickier. I lay on the ground, but this time I don't use a bench. I cross my ankles and bend my legs, then I crunch my hips toward my chest until I feel a contraction and hold for a count of three. These are more difficult, so I limit them to 12-15 reps for three sets.

That's it. If done correctly, crunches will hit the entire ab complex: the serratus, as well as the upper and lower abs. You may want to throw in a slight twisting movement on your crunches from time to time, just to make sure the serratus are getting their due.

As a bodybuilder, don't overdo abdominal training. As outlined earlier, your abs get worked in the process of training other bodyparts, and the last thing you want are abs that are too thick.

AB WORKOUT

EXERCISE	SETS	REPS
Forward crunches	3	20-25
Reverse crunches	3	12-15

92   A PORTRAIT OF DORIAN YATES

CHAPTER 13

LOOK OUT BEHIND YOU! : Back

I treat the back as a two-dimensional entity in which width and thickness should be developed on a complementary basis. Taking that into account, it has to be further understood that the back region is – after thighs – the biggest, most powerful and most complex muscle group of the body. Therefore, I devote a whole workout to it. However, I also include rear delts with my back training. Although rear delts are part of the shoulder structure, they (due to being involved in so many pulling movements) come in for so much work during a back session that I consider the optimum way to train them is during a back workout.

My holistic approach to this bodypart also means I don't compartmentalize back training very much. A lot of bodybuilders confuse the issue by saying that they do a certain exercise for a specific part of the back. It's true that each exercise has its own particular prime function and focuses more on one area than others. But most back exercises – to a greater or lesser degree – hit the total musculature of the back. You can't fire off muscle fibers situated in a specific part of the back without firing off fibers in surrounding areas. An overhead movement like a pulldown puts its greatest stress on the upper lats, and you may feel that area is being worked in isolation. Yet, you're still calling into play other muscles, like the teres major, rhomboids, lower lats and traps. When training, think of the back as a whole entity.

An enduring myth of back training is that using a wide grip when doing a pulldown movement offers the advantage of being able to stretch the lats to a greater degree than is possible with a narrow grip. In fact, the contrary is true. The lats attach at a point adjacent to the armpits and stretch down toward the hips; during exercise, the greater the stretch you can achieve along the whole line of the lats, the greater will be the muscular response. A wide grip shortens the potential length of "stretch," meaning the effect is limited to the upper lats. A close grip lengthens the distance of "stretch" and causes muscular stress throughout the whole of the lats from insertion to insertion. A key ingredient of a great back is the optimum development of the lower lats along the complete length.

My main warm-up for a back workout (following 10 minutes of stationary cycling and a thorough period of stretching) takes the form of two sets of very light barbell rows. Barbell rowing is a basic exercise that hits all sections of the back region. After two sets of 15 reps with 135 pounds, I am ready to commence the formal back workout.

COME ON DOWN

My first back exercise is Hammer Strength machine pulldowns, but you can duplicate this movement by using a conventional lat-pulldown machine. I use a curl grip (as opposed to an overhand grip), because it enables me to get my elbows further back at the midpoint of the movement: This ensures a greater stretch and hence a more extreme muscular contraction. A curl grip also works the upper lats more than the lower lats, so I do this exercise first, since I find that having a pump in the upper lats gives me more stability when doing heavy rows, which are next in my workout.

As the pulldown is the first exercise in my back routine, I do two preliminary sets of 15 and 12 reps, respectively. The second warm-up set will max out at 220 pounds. For my main set, I load up the Hammer Strength machine with 285 pounds.

I grip the overhead handles (or bar for a lat-pulldown machine) and, with my elbows slightly bent, attain a full stretch of the lats by letting my shoulder girdle rise upward. Keeping my elbows slightly bent means that the workload is taken off the biceps and the lats are forced to do the work. Make a mental effort to think of stretching with your lats and not pulling with your arms. You'll find that the effectiveness of your back workouts will improve immeasurably.

Arching my spine and leaning backward only slightly, I pull the machine handles toward me with all the force I can muster, until I feel the muscular contraction bite. I don't have it set in my mind that I must pull back until my elbows are at a predetermined point. It's the contraction taking hold that determines the midpoint. Having said that, the machine handles usually end up near my chin, where I pause for a second and "squeeze" the lats. You're always at your strongest at the point of static contraction. If you can't pause at the midpoint, you must have gotten the weight there by means of momentum and not muscular power.

From the midpoint, I release the load in a slow and controlled fashion, therefore gaining the maximum muscular benefit during the negative part of the rep. On a maximum set, I will typically hit failure at around the eighth to tenth rep, whereupon I will conclude the set with one or two forced reps.

Every second workout, I will do Nautilus pullovers instead of pulldowns. I like the Nautilus pullover setup because it isolates the lats a little more and precludes biceps power from taking over. The style of execution is similar to the pulldown, and the same

Barbell Rows

principles – fully stretching the lats and pulling back to the point of greatest muscle contraction – apply.

MURDERERS' ROW

My second back movement is the barbell row. This is not a "pretty" exercise. It represents an out-and-out mass builder on which I go balls to the wall. I handle as much weight as possible within the parameters of good form. This approach adds slabs of density to all sections of the muscles that form the back complex. I'm overloading, big time, to blitz the muscles into growth. I used to do barbell rows with a curl grip, but since I tore my left biceps doing this exercise in 1994, I've reverted to an overhand grip.

The style I have improvised for this movement digs right into the bellies of the upper-back muscles, while stressing the lower lats to their maximum. When people talk about my all-around back thickness, the barbell row takes the leading credit, and it has been referred to as my exercise.

Although my back muscles are pumped by the previous exercise, I still do a warm-up set of rows. This is because barbell rows bring into play muscles from the lower back, hip and glute areas that have been previously unused in the training session.

For barbell rows, I adopt a position in which my upper body is at a 70-degree angle to the floor. The reason for this is twofold. At an angle of 70 degrees (as opposed to the conventional near-45-degree angle), the lower back is much less susceptible to injury and the lats are placed in a mechanically stronger position. Both of these factors mean that you can use more weight. The heavier the weight, the greater the muscular response.

The whole essence of this exercise – as it is with all of my back movements – is to concentrate on pulling with the lats. With my upper body at a 70-degree angle and my elbows slightly bent, I pull the bar off the floor with all the force I can muster. I ram the bar into my midriff, before controlling the weight as I lower it. When barbell rowing, a lot of people try to use too much weight and cultivate a seesaw motion wherein momentum takes over. During my rows, I try to keep my upper body as still as possible. However, like I said previously, this is not a "pretty" exercise, and handling a very heavy weight means that a slight upper-body movement is likely to occur.

The warm-up for barbell rows comprises 12 reps with 285 pounds. On my main set, I load up the bar with 375 pounds. Typically, I'm looking for eight to ten full-range reps. When I reach the point where I cannot do another full-range rep, I'll do a three-quarter rep and then a half rep to finish. A word of warning: Don't try doing forced reps for barbell rows; besides being extremely difficult and therefore probably unproductive, it's totally unsafe.

SINGLE-ARM ROWS

My third exercise is Hammer Strength machine rows. This machine offers the opportunity to achieve an optimum full-range movement, as opposed to the shorter-range movement that applies to barbell rows. Another advantage is that you can work each lat separately. I used to accomplish that with one-arm dumbbell rows, but once I got to rowing with 215 pounds for 12 reps, I realized that any increase would be impractical, clumsy and ultimately dangerous. The Hammer Strength row machine allowed me to use more weight, which in turn brought the potential for greater muscle gains.

I don't do a warm-up, just one all-out set with 245 pounds on either side of the machine. I complete the set by alternating from arm to arm, one rep at a time. In the starting position, I keep the working arm straight, before pulling until my elbow is as far back as possible without my chest losing contact with the support pad. This position represents the fully contracted point and is achieved without any twist of the upper body. This exercise, with its muscle-isolation properties, allows a controlled and smooth rhythm. When I reach failure, I'll resort to a couple of forced reps, followed occasionally by one or two negative reps.

CABLE ROWS

Next on the agenda are cable rows with a wide overhand grip. This style of cable rowing achieves the goal of thickening the rhomboid and teres major muscles. With my back fully warmed up, I go into one all-out main set. At the start of each rep, I lean slightly forward to fully stretch the lats. Keeping my elbows out, I then pull the bar toward my midriff. This is done with minimum backward sway of the upper torso to ensure that the targeted muscles – and not sheer momentum – take the workload. At the midpoint, I pull my elbows back as far as possible to get the optimum muscle contraction and hold for a count of one. My aim is to complete ten full-range reps, after which I will grind out two forced reps. From time to time, I will finish off with a couple of negative reps.

REAR DELTS

At this point in the workout, I will do my rear-delt work. It acts as the meat in a back-training "sandwich," since I complete the workout with lower-back work after finishing with rear delts.

For my first movement, I move to the Hammer Strength rear-delt machine. No warm-up is necessary, and I jump straight into doing one main set. With my forehead pressed against the support pad, I grip the two handles and pull them back in an arc as far as they will go. At that fully extended position, I will "squeeze" the rear delts before returning slowly to the starting position. However, I do not let the levers return to the point where the weight is released: I want to keep stress on the rear delts throughout the set. Once I hit failure, I will complete two forced reps. On most machine movements, you can do negative reps, but they are not very productive for this exercise since the major stress on the rear delts takes place during the positive, or pulling, part of the rep.

My second and final exercise for rear delts is bent-over dumbbell raises. Seated on the end of a bench, I lean forward and grasp the dumbbells, which are tucked behind my ankles. With my elbows slightly bent and using minimal body movement, I raise the dumbbells up and outward in an arc, until they are at about shoulder level. I'll hold them there for a split-second before slowly returning to the starting position. I aim for eight or ten full reps. When failure is reached, I'll do as many as three partial reps.

IT'S XMAS TIME

The Christmas-tree development I've displayed in my lower-back region has generated a lot of comment throughout my career. I'd love to say that this effect has been achieved through years of noble dedication, or that I have a "secret" exercise that has endowed my physique with this feature. The truth is, the possession of this lower-back characteristic is greatly due to having the genetic muscle structure available in that area in the first place. That genetic disposition is exploited by means of working the lower-back muscles, and it is further highlighted by the attainment of low bodyfat levels after a contest diet.

As far back as the 1986 British Championships, my Christmas tree was clearly visible, although it wasn't as pronounced then, because I didn't have the muscle mass and thickness I do now.

GETTING HYPER

I used to do only deadlifts for my lower back, but the progressively heavier poundages I was using (in order to keep on the overload curve) left me increasingly open to injury. I decided to include hyperextensions as a means of pre-exhausting my lower back before moving on to deadlifts.

I do only one set of hyperextensions. I prefer doing hypers with a barbell across my neck instead of the more traditional method of holding a plate to the chest. The plate-to-chest style feels awkward and doesn't seem to center the stress on the lower back in the precise manner that a barbell across the neck does. With a 40-pound barbell across my neck, I'll do full-range reps to failure. The emphasis is on a strict and full movement, and I hold the position for a count of "one" at the fully contracted position. Twelve to fifteen complete reps in that fashion takes me to failure and brings a deep burn to my lower back.

DEAD LAST

I conclude my back workout with deadlifts. The purpose of this exercise is to thicken the musculature of the whole lower-back region and to bring out full development of the lower lats right down to the point of insertion. For deadlifts, I warm up with 310 pounds for eight reps and then load the bar to 405 pounds for my main set.

The lower back is a very strong but injury-prone area, so I follow textbook style for deadlifts. At the starting position, I keep my head up, my back flat and my knees bent. Then, driving through my hips, I pull the bar upward and concentrate on utilizing only the power of my lats, as I progress to the standing upright position. After a slight pause, I then slowly return the weight to the floor. Eight reps usually take me to failure, and that's it: no partials or anything else. Unlike barbell rows, I'm not looking for any Purple Heart commendations with this exercise.

THE BACK LOT

As I stressed in Chapter Nine, your goal should be to become the best bodybuilder that your physical potential allows. So, while concluding my advice on how to train back, one of the most complex bodyparts, it is worth underscoring the point that you can be only as good as your genetic blueprint permits.

Points of muscle attachment are genetically programmed. You can't, for instance, develop the line of your lats any further down than where they attach to the hip areas. What you can do is fully develop the lats along their complete length so as to make the lower portion thicker and more visible. A lot of bodybuilders have well-developed upper backs, but they exhibit lower backs that are below par. That unbalanced combination destroys the impact of the back when it is viewed (as it is at the judging of a contest) as one entity. In 1990, when I lost to Momo Benaziza at the Night Of Champions, I had good upper-back width, but I lacked Momo's thickness, particularly in my lower lats. After that loss, I began to concentrate on barbell rows, which gave me greater lower-lat thickness. By perpetually analyzing what works and what doesn't for you, you will be able to determine the back routine that will best fulfill your potential.

BACK AND REAR-DELT WORKOUT

EXERCISE	SETS	REPS	POUNDAGE
Hammer Strength pulldowns	1*	15	135
	1*	12	220
	1	8-10	285
or (alternated each workout)			
Nautilus pullovers	1*	15	220
	1*	12	320
	1	8-10	440
Barbell rows	1*	12	285
	1	8-10	375
Hammer Strength one-arm rows	1	8-10	245
Cable rows (overhand grip)	1	8-10	full stack
Hammer Strength rear-delt machine	1	8-10	2 x 55
Bent-over dumbbell raises	1	8-10	2 x 95
Hyperextensions	1	10-12	40
Deadlifts	1*	8	310
	1	8	405

* Warm-up set.

A PORTRAIT OF DORIAN YATES

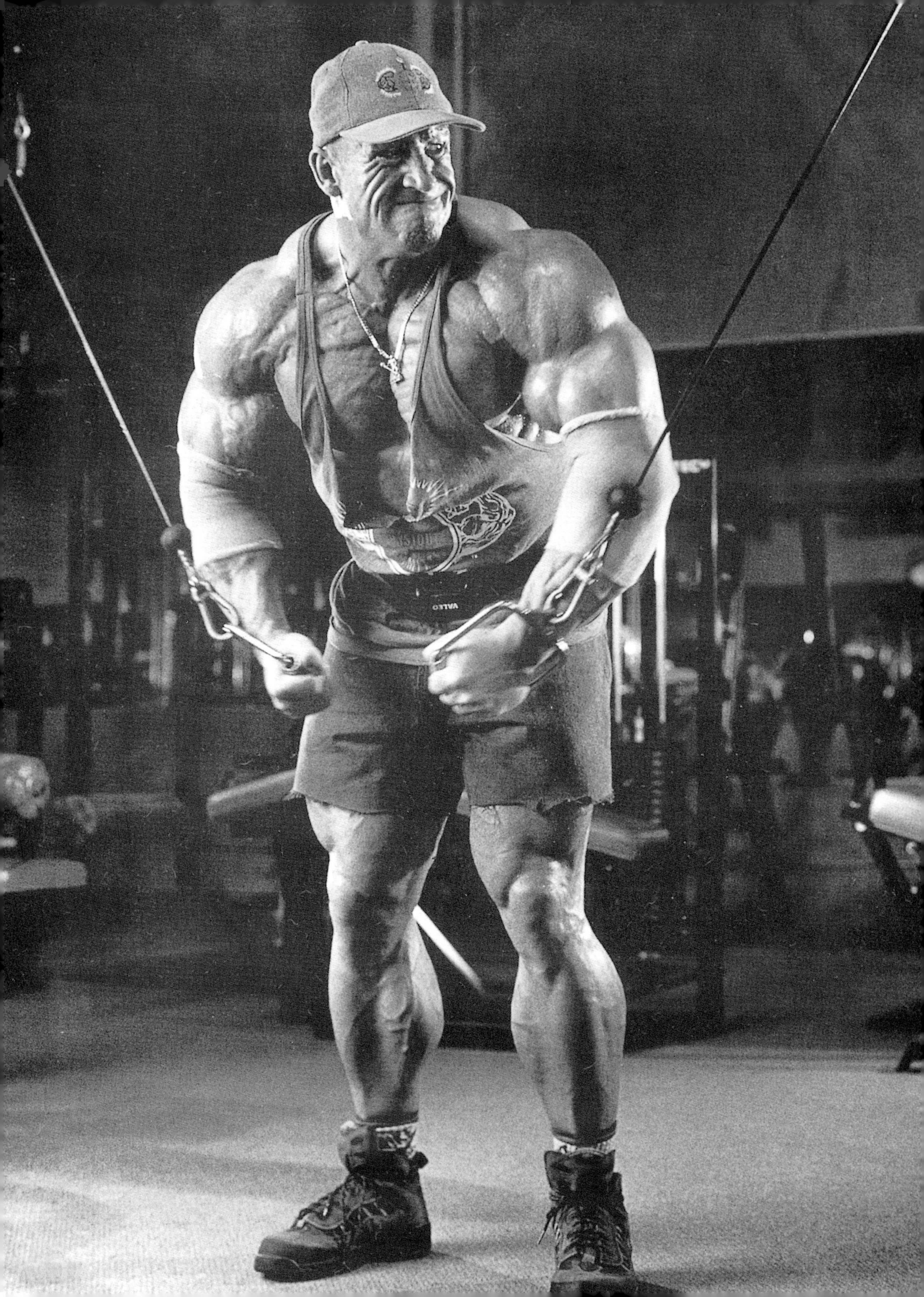

CHAPTER 14

PEC POWER: Chest

Throughout history, a big muscular chest has been representative of masculinity and strength, but, despite that symbolism, pectoral muscles are among the hardest to develop. A major reason is that the type of exercise that stimulates chest growth (a bench press, for instance) is not something you would normally do in everyday life. Even nonbodybuilders know how to mobilize the power of their backs, arms and legs, but recruiting the strength of the chest muscles is not a common out-of-the-gym requirement. Another strike against pecs is that, unlike arms, for instance, it is difficult to see them working and thus it is harder to develop the mind-muscle connection, wherein your mental and physical powers work as one toward a common goal.

To cultivate the mind-muscle connection to fully exploit your chest development, you must first be cognizant of the muscular function of the pecs. Pectoral muscles help bring the arms up and down (pressing movements) and/or across the body (flye-type movements). To add muscle to your pecs, you must concentrate on those two types of movements. To further stress the pecs while they are completing those movements, you must execute each rep of each exercise with strict style. You must make the pec muscles do all the work, not employ unrealistic poundages that force you to cheat the movement.

On the subject of ego-training, the most abused exercise when it comes to "let's load up the bar and to hell with style and function" is the flat-bench press. The root of this mania lies in one of the most common questions asked of bodybuilders: "What can you bench?" From that derives the macho approach of being more concerned with what's on the bar than with what effect it has on pectoral stimulation. For the record, I use four exercises in my chest routine and the flat-bench press is not one of them.

BENCH THE BENCH

While many people obtain good results from the flat-bench press, I do not feel it is the best major mass-builder for the chest. When flat benching, I find that the power of the front delts intrudes too much and takes a lot of the stress off the pec muscles. Another negative is that the angle of flat benching puts the pec tendons in a very vulnerable injury-prone position. A lot of the torn-pec injuries sustained in bodybuilding have occurred as a result of doing heavy flat-bench presses.

INCLINED TO INCLINES

It is my opinion that incline and decline presses are better chest stimulators than the flat-bench variety, as well as being safer. As regards incline and decline work, it is often said that the former is for the upper-pec area and the latter is for the lower-pec region. I don't agree with that: In comparison to flat-bench presses, the incline and decline versions afford a much fuller range of movement, which in turn means they are superior for generating all-around pec development. My personal choice as the principal mass builder for pecs is the incline press.

For this exercise, I set the bench at an angle of 30 degrees: any steeper and the front delts are called into play too much. Because chest is a large bodypart and I will be using quite a bit of weight for my main set of incline benches, I do three warm-up sets. The first set is twelve reps with a very light weight; the second is ten reps with about half my main-set weight; and the final warm-up set is eight comfortable reps with about 70% of my main-set weight. Settling myself onto the bench, I take a grip about six inches wider (each side) than shoulder width, and I visualize moving the bar through a full range of motion. That means lowering the bar to touch my upper pecs, before, without bouncing it, pressing it back to arms' length. At that fully extended position, I tense my pecs for a full muscular contraction. To achieve full muscular contraction, imagine that you are trying to push your pecs together. When I reach failure, I'll most often go on to complete two forced reps, although I'll finish off with a couple of rest-pause reps from time to time.

SEATED FOR THE BENCH

My second exercise is Hammer Strength seated bench presses. If you don't have access to the Hammer Strength version, most gyms have some form of seated bench-press machine. This movement is a compound mass-builder like the incline bench press, but it affords two extra options. First, it puts the pecs under stress from a different angle than the overhead barbell exercise; and second, because you don't have to worry about balancing a free weight, it allows you to isolate the pecs more and concentrate on achieving a full contraction of the pecs.

Due to my chest being pumped by the incline work, only one warm-up set of ten reps is necessary in preparation for my main set of seated bench presses. With my back braced against the support pad, I concentrate on keeping the whole of my body – with the exception of my arms – still throughout the set. I press out to the fully extended position, and get a great burn as I complete a full contraction of my pecs. At the failure point, my partner will help me achieve two forced reps, or I'll finish with a

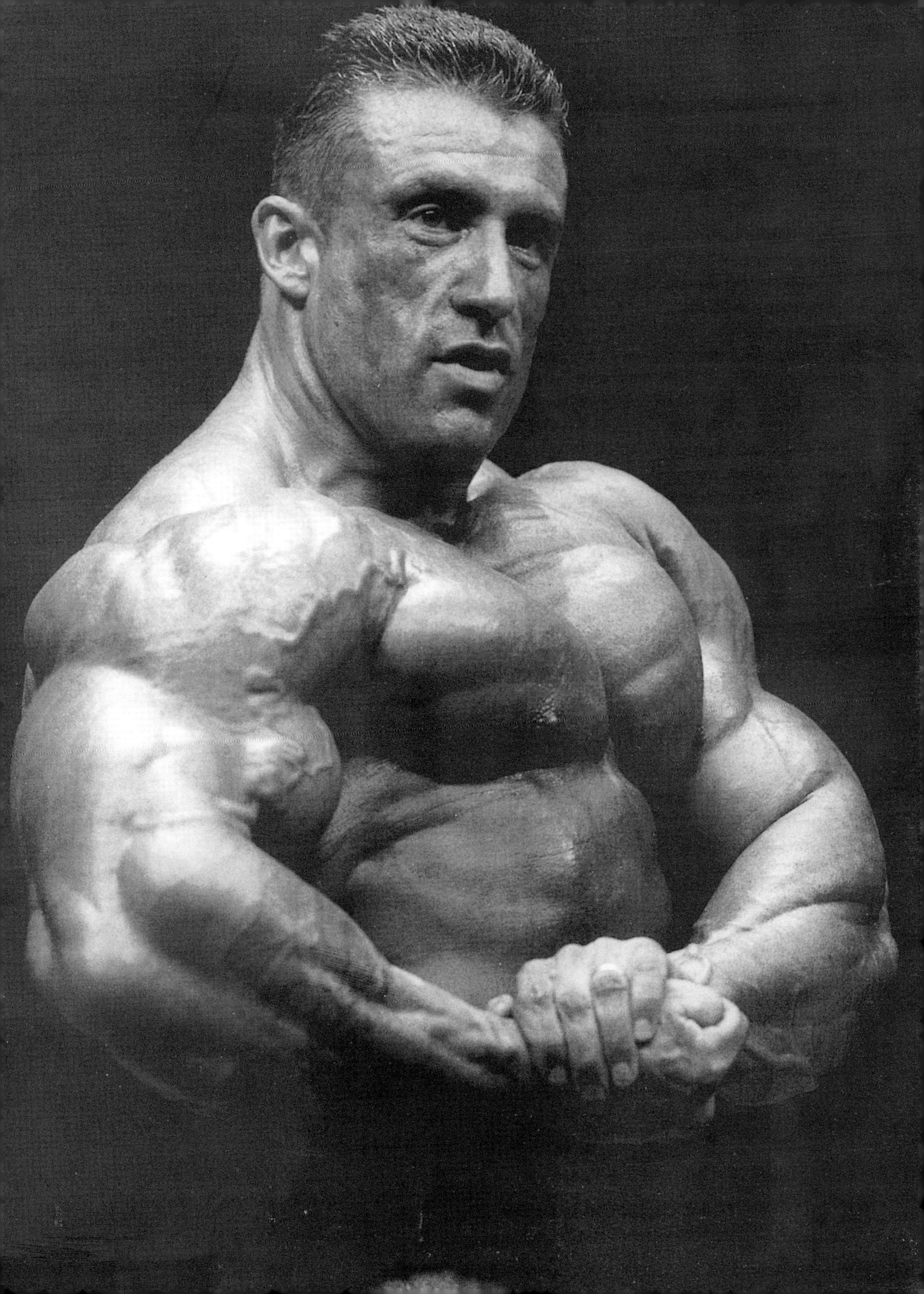

couple of rest-pause reps. Other times, I use this machine to do a couple of negative reps, wherein my partner helps me press the weight to the fully extended position, from where I resist the weight as much as possible as it returns to the starting position.

COME FLYE WITH ME

I next turn to incline dumbbell flyes, which work the middle and outer areas of the pecs. This is an extreme exercise, where the quality and technique of the movement should take precedence over using heavy weights. I'll do one warm-up set of ten reps to get into the groove of the movement, and then I move on to my main set.

Starting with the dumbbells held overhead at arms' length, I slowly begin to lower them in an outward arc. As I begin the lowering process, I'll bend my elbows slightly and keep them locked in that position throughout the set. From then on, it's a case of mimicking the action of hugging of a tree. Maintaining a controlled style, I bring my elbows down as far as possible and get a good stretch at that lower position. At the top, I don't bring the dumbbells together; to do so would release the tension on the pecs. Instead, without the dumbbells touching, I squeeze my pecs for a full muscular contraction. When I hit failure, my partner will cup his hands under my elbows and help me pump out a couple of forced reps. Alternatively, I'll drop the dumbbells and do five or six reps with a lighter pair of dumbbells in descending-set fashion.

CROSSOVERS

As a contest draws nearer, I'll include one set of cable crossovers as my final pec exercise. With my chest muscles almost totally spent by the previous workload, crossovers (an isolation exercise) offers a final touch of digging deep into the pecs to encourage the degree of separation needed on a contest stage. Beginners and intermediates don't need to do this exercise on a regular basis: You'd be better advised to concentrate on compound movements like presses or dips.

Grasping the crossover handles, I stand in the middle of the pulley apparatus and bend slightly forward from the waist: This stance offers stability to the movement. Keeping my elbows slightly bent, I let the handles rise to about shoulder height, before slowly pushing down. As I push down, I "crunch" the pecs; the style of execution is somewhat similar to hitting a most-muscular pose. Throughout the set, the tension on the pecs is constant; by the time I reach failure (around the twelfth rep), my pecs are burning. At that point, I'll conclude with three or four partial reps and my chest workout is over.

MIND-MUSCLE

In the pecking order of muscle groups, chest is one of the most powerful and rates membership as one of the "Big Three" along with back and legs. However, as stated at the beginning of this chapter, it is one of the hardest to fully develop. For optimum progress, concentrate on the quality of movement and the quality of each rep. Cultivate the mind-muscle connection: Visualize your pecs growing as you complete each rep. When training chest – and this applies to all muscle groups – it is not the amount of weight you have on the bar that is important, it is the effect of that weight on the muscle. Maximum muscular response is obtained from the shock of high-intensity, high-quality training. Make sure to use textbook style and a full range of motion. Lock those components into your program and increases in muscle size and power will be yours.

CHEST WORKOUT

EXERCISE	SETS	REPS	POUNDAGE
Incline barbell presses	1*	12	135
	1*	10	220
	1*	8	310
	1	8	425
Hammer Strength seated bench presses	1*	10	220
"	1	6-8	350
Incline dumbbell flyes	1*	10	2 x 75
"	1	8	2 x 110
Cable crossovers	1	10-12	2 x 90

* Warm-up set

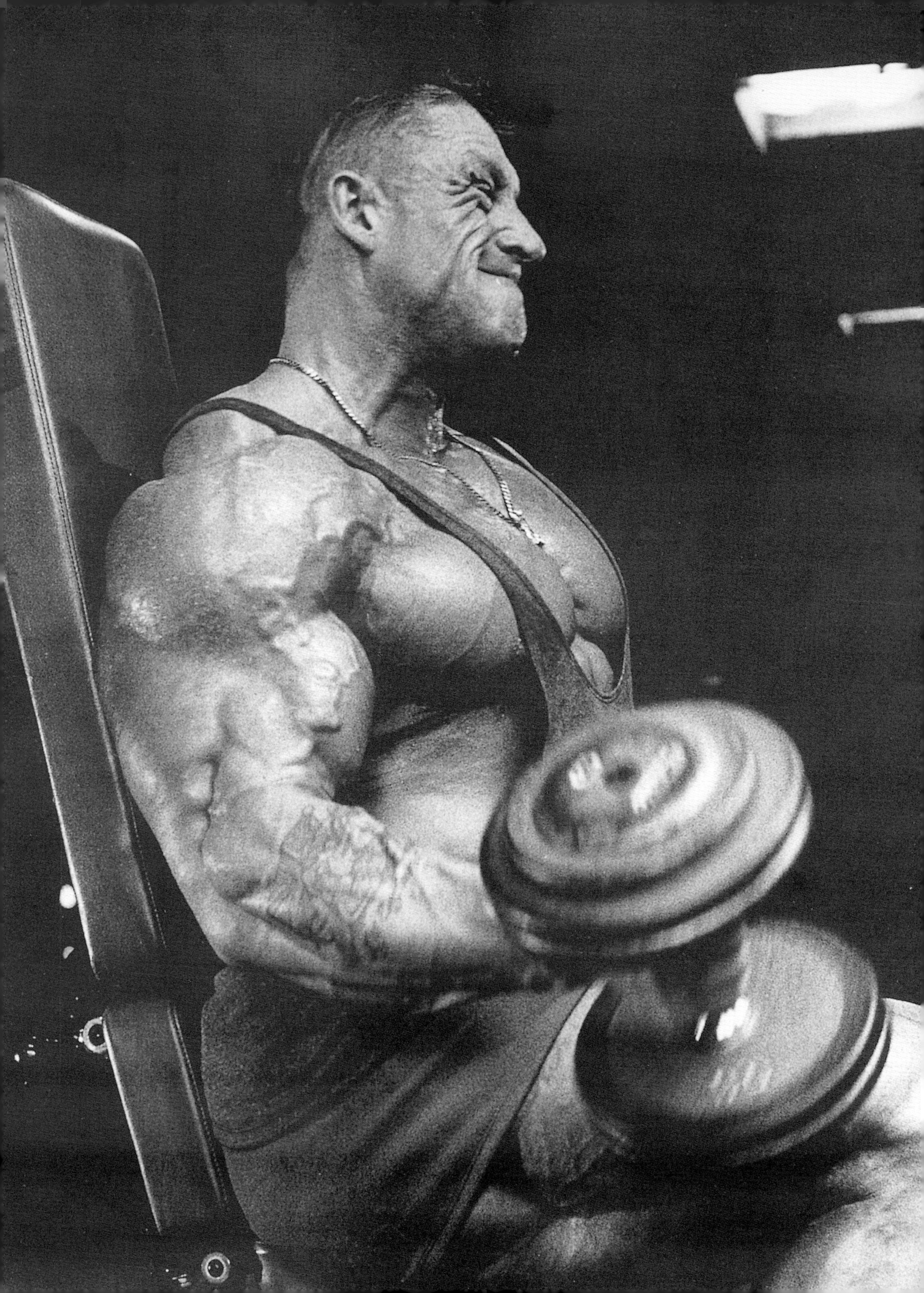

CHAPTER 15

SMOKIN' GUNS: Biceps

In comparison to bodyparts like thighs and back, the biceps is relatively small, but by virtue of being the showpiece bodybuilding muscle, it is by far the most overtrained muscle group. Every bodybuilder wants to maximize biceps development, but subjecting it to the type of workload accorded larger muscle groups is a certain passport to zero biceps growth.

The biceps muscle has two functions: to rotate the forearm and to bend the arm at the elbow joint. Because of its small size and limited range of movement, you don't need a vast range of exercises for optimum development as you do with intricate bodyparts like the back, which you need to hit from a variety of angles. Nevertheless, numerous bodybuilders ill-advisedly grind out set after set of biceps work. My view is that all the biceps require to potentiate growth is minimal sets of three different movements per workout.

Because I believe the biceps are the most overtrained and abused muscle group, I'm using this chapter to not only explain how I train them, but also to highlight a number of bodybuilding no-nos. These transgressions are most frequently committed against biceps, but they can also apply to other bodyparts.

DON'T TRAIN YOUR EGO

Handling too much weight during biceps training equates to exercising your ego instead of your muscle fibers. Besides being unproductive in a muscle-building sense, such an overambitious approach carries a high risk of injury. The cheating principle has its place in a bodybuilder's repertoire (only after failure has been reached), but many individuals start cheating from the first rep during a heavy set of barbell curls. They employ incorrect technique in order to handle excess poundage; they lean back like a limbo-dancer to wrestle the weight through the completion of the set. This style of execution not only invites a probability of injury, but also takes the stress off the muscle being worked, which is the whole point of the exercise.

DON'T OVERDO INTENSITY

When it comes to intensity techniques, the Golden Rule is that the smallish biceps muscle group should not be placed on a par with its larger "brothers" like thighs and back. For an all-out set on back, I work to failure and, then on occasion, will go through the full gamut of forced reps, followed by partial reps, before finishing with negative or rest-pause reps. Expanding the intensity threshold with these techniques is not effective for a small muscle group.

For an all-out biceps set, I usually reach failure around the six to eight reps mark, do one or two forced reps and then finish the set. Other times I'll go to failure, put the weight down, rest for 10 seconds, and do another two reps in rest-pause fashion, or I'll kick in with a descending set. What I never do is hammer my biceps past the orthodox failure point as I would with a large bodypart like back.

Overdoing biceps with forced and negative reps puts too much stress on the fragile joint and muscle-fiber structure of this bodypart. Also, pushing a smaller muscle too much can adversely affect the central nervous system, which can make you feel irritated and disrupt your sleep pattern. These are classic signs of overtraining. For beginners and intermediates, training to failure is all the biceps require.

DON'T SKIMP ON RECUPERATION

Many bodybuilders train biceps two or even three times a week. However, my experience is that it takes anywhere between four and seven days before the biceps recuperate fully from a workout. I currently train my biceps once every seven days.

What must also be taken into account is the stress placed on the biceps during a back routine. Because of the many pulling movements endemic to training back, the biceps get quite a workout as secondary muscles. That factor, compounded by a volume-training strategy during a designated biceps workout, can be a sure route to burnout. In fact, because biceps undergo so much indirect stress while working other bodyparts, I'll occasionally skip a biceps workout completely if I detect signs of overtraining. That means I'll sometimes go two weeks without working them. I can't emphasis this point enough: You can't hammer a small muscle group like you can a large one.

The other side of the biceps coin is that you can employ a pretty brisk pace when working out. This is because you don't sustain the same degree of oxygen debt or assault on the nervous system performing, for instance, dumbbell curls as you do after completing an all-out set of leg presses.

DON'T TRY TO REWRITE NATURE

It's common to hear guys say they've structured a routine that will give them a Robby Robinson-

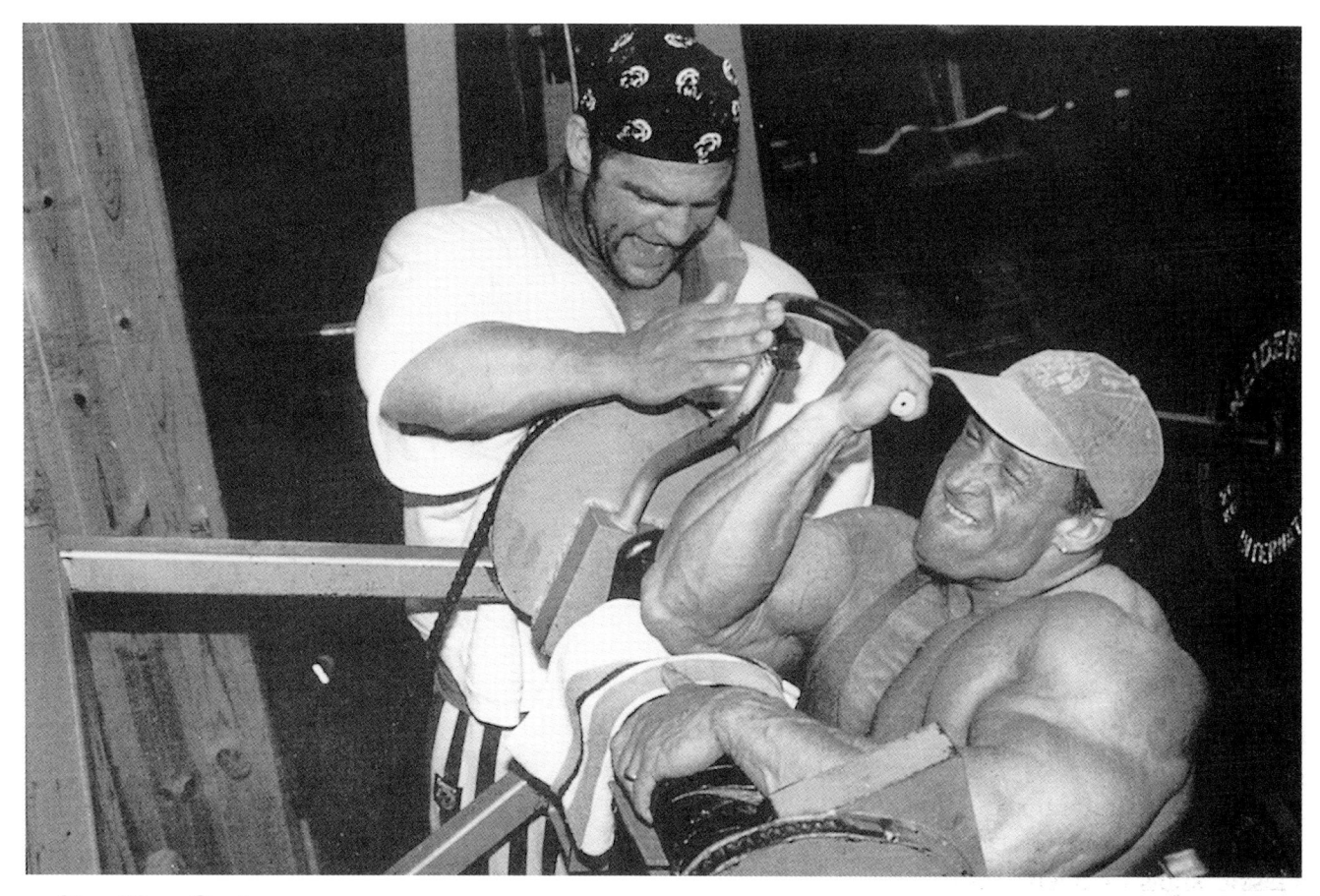

Nautilus Curls

type peak to their biceps, but unless you were born with biceps muscle insertions similar to Robby's, duplication of his fabulous biceps peak is impossible.

Basically, there are two heads to the biceps: a short and long head. Various movements hit each one. If you concentrate on working only one head, you may slightly alter the overall look of the biceps, but as far as muscle length (the point at which muscle fibers attach to the tendons) is concerned, you're stuck with what Mother Nature gave you. If you've got a short biceps, you'll always have a short biceps.

Some people believe that movements like preacher curls will extend biceps length. This exercise can help develop size in the lower biceps, but only where the muscle fibers already exist; they won't lengthen the insertions of those fibers.

DON'T FORGET THE BRACHIALIS

The brachialis is the muscle on the outer arm between the triceps and biceps. Its development adds a complete and powerful look to the upper arm and is best isolated by movements such as hammer curls and reverse barbell curls. To kick-start the brachialis, I suggest you do a couple of sets of either of those exercises at the conclusion of your biceps workout. I currently maintain brachialis size by doing EZ-curl barbell curls, in which the angle of the underhand grip ensures that stress is placed on the brachialis.

THE 10-MINUTE BICEPS WORKOUT

My biceps work follows my chest program, but although my physiological system is warmed up, I still take a few minutes to stretch my biceps. In addition, as a general biceps warm-up, I do 30 reps of dumbbell curls with a pair of 20-pound dumbbells. My official biceps workout comprises 5 sets spread over 3 exercises and takes about 10 minutes to complete.

SO INCLINED

I believe in doing an isolation dumbbell movement first for biceps, followed by a compound barbell movement. This procedure pre-exhausts the biceps with the first exercise, so that during the second compound movement, biceps strength will give out first.

My chosen isolation movement is incline dumbbell curls, which I do with both arms at a time instead of the more traditional alternate method. Curling the dumbbells together means the actual training time is shorter and the intensity is more concentrated. It also negates the twisting stress on the lower back caused by single curls, and makes it harder to cheat. With single-arm curls, you may find yourself maneuvering your torso into a position where it can help you cheat out the last couple of tough reps. Using two arms eliminates that tendency.

I'll warm up with a set of eight reps before moving on to my main set. Using strict form, I'll slowly pump out six to eight reps to failure, and then I'll either drop the weights and immediately pick up a lighter set of dumbbells and grind out another four or five reps (in descending-sets fashion), or I'll let my partner help me complete a couple of forced reps.

EZ DOES IT

I used to favor the standard barbell curl as my second and heaviest biceps exercise, but after tearing my right biceps in 1994, I resorted to the EZ-curl bar version. The less severe angle of grip afforded by the EZ-curl bar reduces strain on the tendons of the biceps. It also carries the bonus of giving the brachialis a workout. After a warm-up set with a moderate poundage I'm ready for my main set.

With the bar loaded, I concentrate on the quality and intensity of the movement and don't cheat. My style of execution is controlled and deliberate. I keep my wrists locked throughout each rep to immobilize forearm strength — I want the biceps to do all the work. At the uppermost point of the rep, I pause and tense the biceps for a full muscular contraction. I usually eke out eight full-range reps before failure. At that point, I like to complete one or two forced reps. Other times, after having reached failure, I put the bar down for 10 seconds, then curl for one or two more reps in rest-pause fashion. I don't believe in stressing the biceps for too many reps past the failure point. At that stage, I'm not firing the muscle fibers; the stress is mainly on the nervous system.

For those training alone and unable to do forced reps, you can employ the aforementioned rest-pause principle or use the descending-sets principle, whereby, after reaching failure, you strip off some weight from the bar or pick up a lighter weight.

NAUTILUS

My final exercise is unilateral Nautilus curls. For those who don't have access to this type of machine, you can substitute one-arm dumbbell preacher curls or dumbbell concentration curls. The Nautilus curl is an isolation exercise. I use it as a finishing exercise for the biceps, in which the intensity pushes that final flush of blood into the muscle.

Due to the biceps work just completed, there's no need for a warm-up on the Nautilus. I do just one main set with each arm. Again, style is super-strict, as I slowly curl the weight and, at the midpoint, squeeze for a full muscular contraction before slowly returning to the start position. Between the sixth to eighth rep I'll reach failure, then my partner will help me achieve two forced reps.

Ten minutes after starting my biceps workout, I'm finished, while some guys would be only a fraction into their 20-sets-for-biceps regimen.

A FINAL "BI" LINE

If you hit a sticking point with your biceps training, or any bodypart, the solution doesn't lie in employing more sets and reps. The answer will derive from dissecting the problem and then working out a strategy to solve it. Let me give you an example

In 1987 I hit a rut with my biceps development. I figured out that the problem was due to the fact that my biceps were genetically weaker than my front-delt and forearm muscles, which were assuming an unacceptable part of the workload as interrelated muscles. Consequently, I devised methods that negated the power of my forearms and front delts during my biceps routine. As a result, I overcame my sticking point. The solution was two-pronged: To reduce the influence of my forearms, I kept my wrists rigid during biceps work; and to remove my front delts from the exercise, I adopted a strict upright style with no swaying of my upper torso.

Whatever problem you may encounter, analyze the situation, then mentally focus throughout each set on the solution to the problem. Cultivating the mind-muscle connection is invaluable, especially with regard to problem areas.

BICEPS WORKOUT

EXERCISE	SETS	REPS	POUNDAGE
Incline dumbbell curls	1*	10	2 x 50 *
	1	6-8	2 x 70
EZ-curl barbell curls	1*	10	100
	1	6-8	140
Nautilus curls	1	6-8	120

A PORTRAIT OF DORIAN YATES

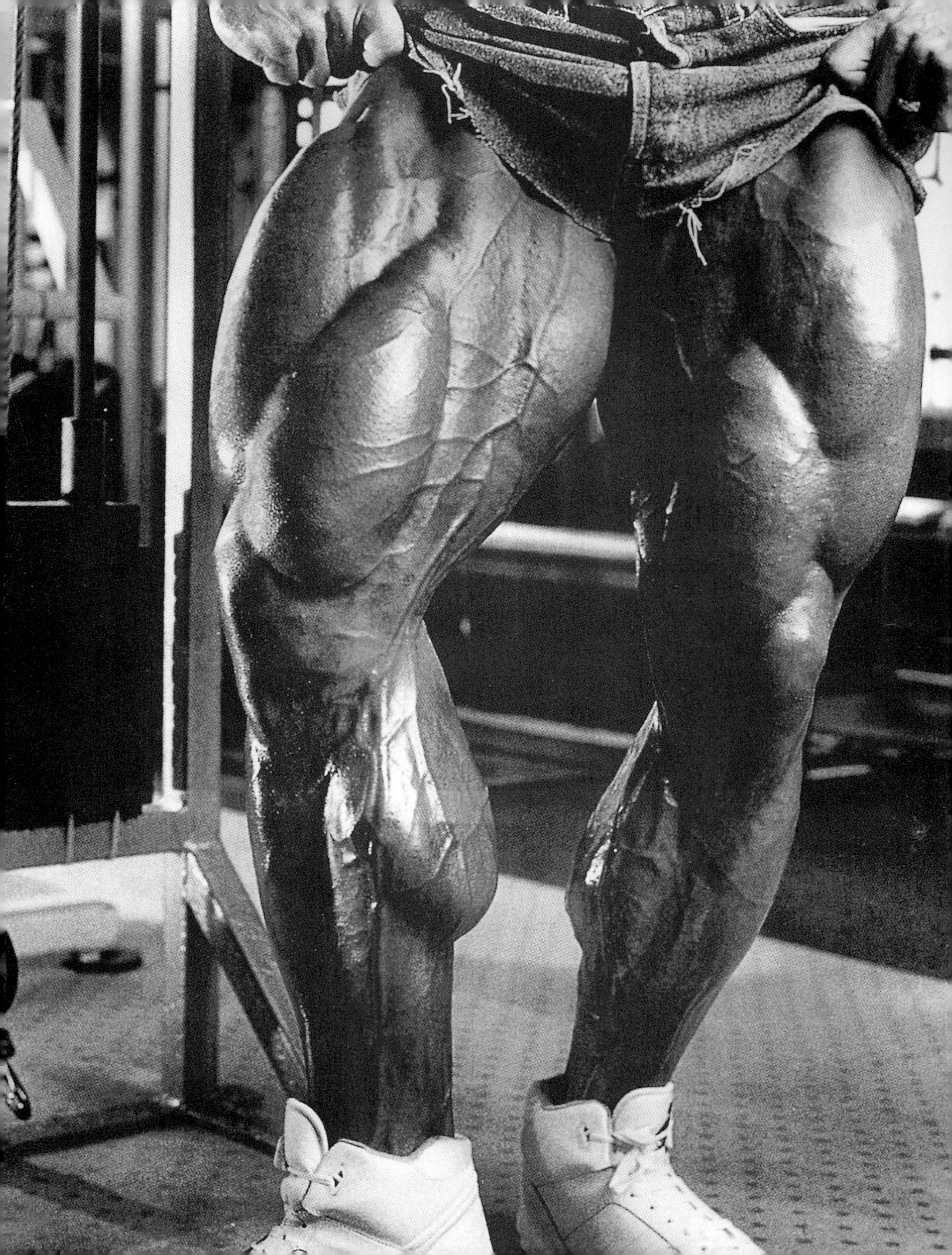

CHAPTER 16

THE WORKOUT FROM HELL:
Quads, Hamstrings and Calves

The amalgam of quadriceps, hamstrings and calves comprises the biggest and most powerful muscle network of the human physique. Legs constitute half the body, and, because the demands for their development are so extensive and intensive, I devote a whole workout to them.

What I aim for in my leg training is ultimate mass, in tandem with deep separation, detail and rock-hard density — that means sweeping, cut thighs, hanging striated hamstrings, and full and split calves. To achieve that look, you have to be prepared to give every last ounce of effort in the gym. Training legs ain't pretty and it truly separates the men from the boys, both in the gym and onstage. But lest you think I fear or even dread leg workouts, the opposite is true: I get fired up by the challenge of a leg workout. The bigger the challenge, the more inspired I am.

There really hasn't been a major restructuring to my leg training since I began bodybuilding in 1983. It's been a case of arriving at a formula and then fine-tuning it step-by-step as I learned what worked and what didn't. The only radical change was my decision to abandon free-standing barbell squats back in 1989. I'd always loved the challenge of heavy, full-range barbell squats, but this exercise caused the hip injury that nearly ended my career in 1987. As I got stronger and my poundage increased, the movement became more awkward, and was putting excessive and dangerous stress on my hip girdle. I was getting a lot of minor strains and tweaks.

I persevered with the exercise until October of 1989, when I finally accepted that my structure — narrow hips, longish legs — was not ideal for heavy barbell squats. Instead, I began to rely on leg presses and Smith machine squats as mass builders for thighs. However, I still recommend that everyone, beginners in particular, earn their thigh-building spurs with barbell squats. You should cease doing them only if you feel, as I did, that they're causing more harm than good.

The other change in my leg training is that I have increased my reps during my main sets. Initially, I would max out at around six-to-eight reps, but I now aim for 12 full reps to failure on most leg movements. I feel that legs, by virtue of the heavy workload, can absorb and actually need that extra prolonged intensity in comparison to other bodyparts. While increasing the rep range, I also began to execute each rep in a slower and more precise style than the explosive method I used to favor.

A thorough warm-up is important before commencing any bodypart workout, and it is especially crucial before launching into a leg routine. My preparation encompasses 10 minutes on a stationary bike, followed by a series of stretching movements such as splits and hurdlers' stretches.

EXHAUSTING EXTENSIONS

My first thigh exercise is leg extensions. This is an isolation exercise for the quads and serves as a more comprehensive warm-up. Plus, leg extensions act as pre-exhaust movement for the heavy compound exercises (e.g., leg presses, machine squats and hack squats) to come. What I'm doing is fatiguing the quad muscles with extensions, so that on the compound movements, I am forced to use less weight than if my muscles were fresh. This means, on compound movements, that I still apply the utmost stress to the thigh muscles and take them to the limit, but still reduce the skeletal stress on the hip and knee joints and lower back.

My first set of leg extensions is a light one with 15 reps, followed by a second set with moderate weight for 12 reps. All reps are executed in super-strict and controlled style — there is no squirming in the seat or swinging the weight from momentum. Nothing should take over the workload from the front thighs. At the fully extended position, I pause for a second and then tense the quad muscles to gain a full muscular contraction. For my main set, I choose a weight that will induce failure at between the 10th and 12th rep. Once I have reached failure, my partner will help me complete two forced reps.

MAKING THE PRESS ACCOUNTABLE

For stimulating sheer quad mass, the leg press is my exercise of choice. Beware, however, because it is one of the most abused and misused exercises in the bodybuilding repertoire. The sport abounds with erroneous claims from guys citing leg-press poundages in excess of 1,500 pounds. These guys may indeed have 1,500 pounds loaded on the machine, but they certainly aren't using a full range of motion. What most of these guys do is set the supporting backboard at such an extreme upright angle that their knees can only move four or five inches during their so-called "reps." They're doing only a partial movement and, thus, achieving only a partial stimulation of the thigh muscles.

To really dig deep into the muscles, from insertion to insertion, you need to employ a full range of motion. This is achieved by setting the backboard at a relatively low angle: one that allows you to open up the angle between your upper and lower torso, so that you can bring your knees to a point where they almost touch your chest.

I do a couple of warm-up sets of 12 reps each, and then load the machine up to 1,200 pounds or more to do my main set. I perform each rep in a slow and deliberate style, focusing on obtaining a complete and full range of motion. I keep the weight moving and keep the stress on the muscles, as I move smoothly through the negative-to-positive transition. Once I've reached failure on my main set, I do a couple of rest-pause reps, and then hobble away from the machine.

With regard to foot positions for thigh exercises, I don't worry too much about the premise that says pointing your toes outward or inward will hit a different area of the quads. The foot position that feels most comfortable will be the one that allows you to exert the most power — the whole point of the game, after all — and bring forth the most muscle dividends.

As an alternative to leg presses, I sometimes do Smith machine squats. Here, again, the emphasis is on textbook execution, minus the explosive burst, while completing a full range of motion. My stance is just a bit narrower than shoulder width. To reduce the recruitment of my glutes and lower back, I place my feet directly under the bar. The workload of reps and sets is the same as for leg presses, with the main set concluding with a couple of rest-pause reps.

A PORTRAIT OF DORIAN YATES

116   A PORTRAIT OF DORIAN YATES

A PORTRAIT OF DORIAN YATES 117

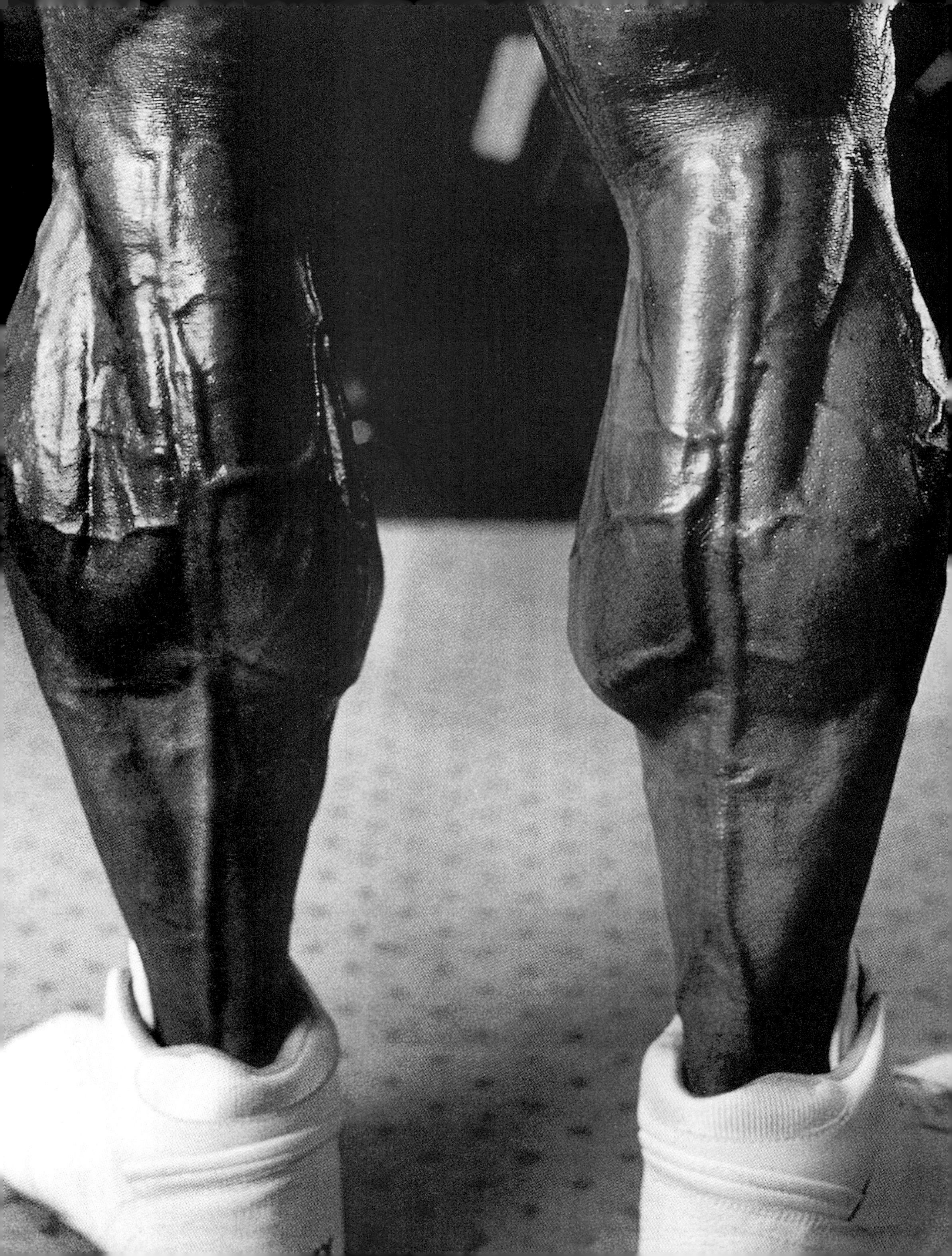

HACKING IT

I use hack squats to generate outer-thigh sweep. Since my quads are pretty well pumped by the time I get to this exercise, I do just one warm-up set of 12 reps. I employ a stance with my heels fairly close together and make sure each rep is executed in a controlled manner. I descend slowly to a point where my butt is as low as it can get, and then without any "bouncing," I smoothly push back to the starting position. I hit failure around the 12th rep, after which I finish off with a couple of rest-pause reps.

FRIED HAMS

I start the hamstring segment of my workout with lying leg curls. I do one warm-up set of 10 to 12 reps. To achieve maximum isolation and stress on the hamstrings, I concentrate on keeping my front thighs and hips flat to the bench. The style of execution is slow and controlled as I raise my heels, and, when I reach the top position, I hold and tense the hamstrings for a maximum contraction. I then lower the weight slowly to keep maximum tension on the hams throughout the rep. Once I reach failure, my partner will help me complete two forced reps.

DEADLY FORCE

My next exercise is stiff-legged deadlifts. I go straight into my main set and aim for eight to ten complete reps. Using wrist straps, I grasp the bar with an overhand grip, with my hands spaced slightly narrower than shoulder width. For me, the phrase "stiff-legged" is a misnomer because I bend my knees slightly. This variation still accomplishes the goal of maintaining tension on the hams, but takes the stress off the tendons at the back of the knees.

I begin by lifting the bar to mid-shin level — this constitutes the start of the rep and the point where the hams take over. Keeping my head up and my back straight, I concentrate on using my hams as levers in pulling the weight to the standing upright position. At that point, I don't lean back and roll the shoulders as you would with a standard deadlift — doing that would release the tension on the hams. Instead, I slowly return to the mid-shin position, and, without bouncing the weight, start the next rep. Once I reach failure between the eighth-and-tenth rep, the set is over. The mechanics of this exercise doesn't lend itself to forced reps, etc., so I end there.

STAND-UP EXERCISE

My final hamstring exercise is standing leg curls. Because of the downward gravity involved in its execution, this exercise helps carve out the separation between the glutes and hamstrings. Obviously, these have to be done one limb at a time. Again, my style is slow and deliberate, as I bring my heel up toward my butt. Once that point is reached, I pause and tense the muscle for a full contraction. One set of 10 to 12 reps for each hamstring completes the job.

NO-BULL CALVES

I conclude my leg workout with calf training. I was blessed with good calf genetics, but that doesn't mean I can afford to slack off when training them. My credo on calf training is to hit them as intensely as possible with the minimum amount of sets and exercises.

The exercises I use are standing calf raises, which zone in on the gastrocnemius (the upper, larger segment of the calf muscle), and seated calf raises, which accentuate the soleus (the smaller lower head). With both, I'm aiming for a set that maxes out between 10 to 12 reps. I'm not a believer in doing high-rep sets for calves. You basically do high-rep calf work all day just by walking around, so it doesn't seem logical that they'll be shocked into growth by a similar volume approach in the gym.

When doing standing calf raises, keep your legs slightly bent to minimize pressure on the knee joints. I complete one warm-up set, followed by one heavy set to failure. The style of execution is slow and deliberate. I go as far down as my ankle flexibility will allow, and then pause for a split second to get a maximum stretch. From here, I slowly push upward until I'm standing on my toes, then pause again to put the muscle under optimum stress. By the time I've reached failure, my calves are burning, and there's no need for any rest-pause reps or any other intensity techniques.

With my calves fully warmed up, I go straight into my main set of seated calf raises. Keeping my toes pointed forward, I grind out the necessary reps, making sure I do it in a precise and controlled fashion, while achieving a full range of motion — heels all the way down and all the way up to somewhere between 10 to 12 reps. After that, the whole leg workout is finally over.

IMPORTANT ADVICE

Within the preceding chapters, I've outlined the exercises and techniques that have worked for me. I believe that with honest application, my training philosophy will work for the vast majority, but not down to the last rep. Remember, we are all individuals with individual needs and reactions. You may be structurally unsuited to a certain exercise, or perhaps you may find that with a particular bodypart, a higher- or lower-rep range works best for you. You must monitor your progress and be prepared to change, modify and/or improvise if you feel you are not fully benefiting from my program. That being said, I'm a great believer in the KIS principle: Keep It Simple. If you're making progress, stick to your program. If you're not progressing, isolate the problem and solve it by consistently analyzing your workouts and diet.

Have confidence in your own ability to judge what is happening to your body, and then make sensible decisions based on that feedback. Bodybuilding is an ongoing process — you should be constantly selecting, rejecting, modifying and learning as you search for the pieces that fit the unique jigsaw puzzle of your body. Some of the things I suggest in this book will have to be adjusted because they may not work for you. Don't blindly follow what I say just because I'm Mr. Olympia. You are bodybuilding for you, not Dorian Yates.

LEG WORKOUT

Warm-up: 10 minutes on a stationary bike, followed by gentle stretching of all muscle groups to be trained.

	EXERCISE	SETS	REPS	POUNDAGE
QUADS	Leg extensions	1*	15	130
		1*	12	200
		1	10-12	270
	Leg presses	1*	12	770
		1*	12	1,045
		1	10-12	1,265
	Hack squats	1*	12	440
		1	10-12	660
HAMSTRINGS	Lying leg curls	1*	10-12	130
		1	10-12	180
	Stiff-legged deadlifts	1	8-10	350
	Single-leg curls	1	8-10	50
CALVES	Standing calf raises	1*	10-12	900
		1	10-12	1,300
	Seated calf raises	1	10-12	250

* Warm-up sets

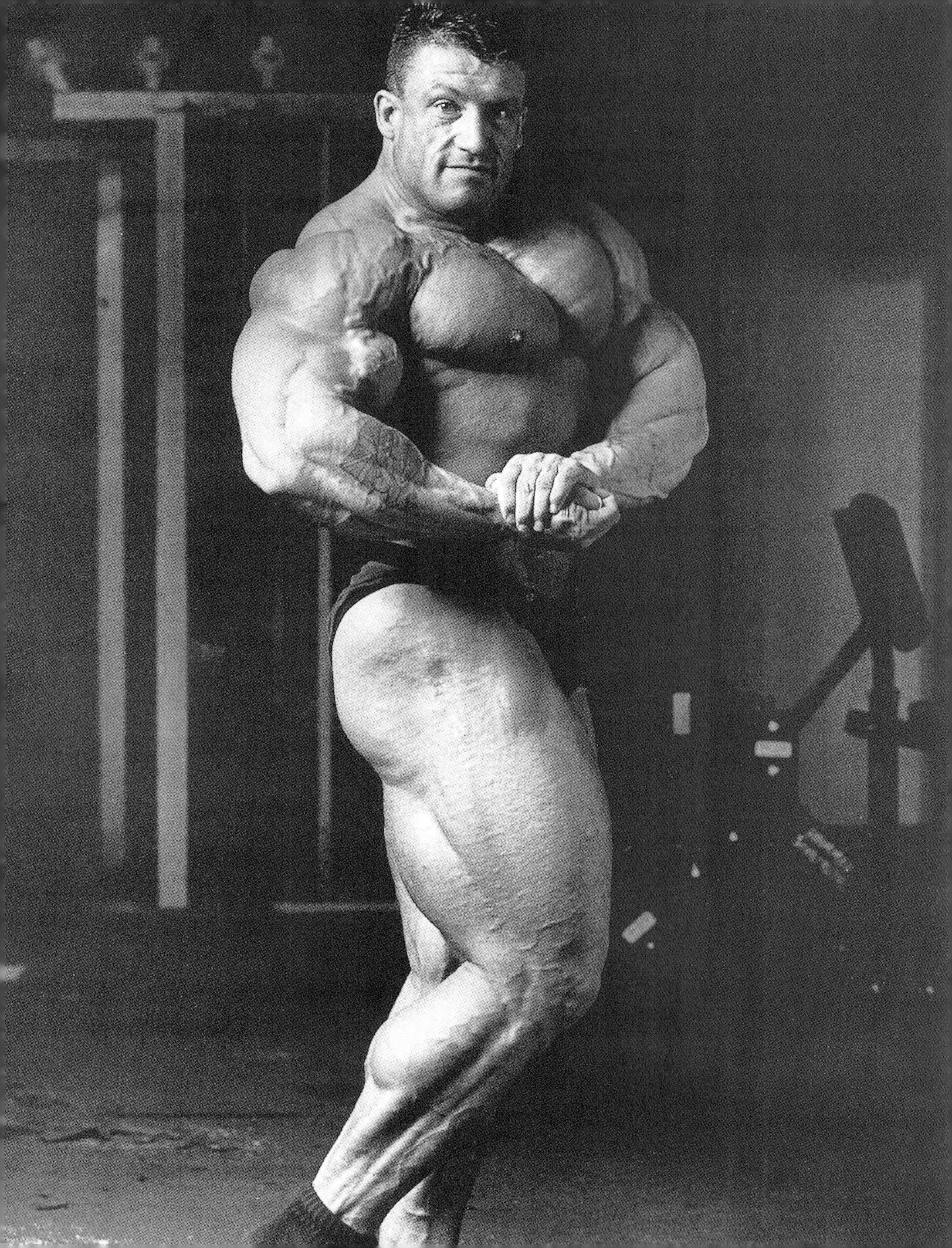

CHAPTER 17

NUTRITION FOR MASS

It has been said that correct nutrition can be as much as 80% responsible for a bodybuilder's success. I don't go along with that reasoning. To my mind, bodybuilding is a four-way fusion of correct training, correct nutrition, correct recuperation and correct mental approach.

Training is the initial kick-start stimulus, nutrition and recuperation fuel the effect of that stimulus, and a positive mental attitude is the glue that holds the whole mechanism together. All four are interrelated and dependent on each other. Deny or shortchange yourself of any one of those four elements and the whole entity collapses.

It is easy to see why the 80% nutrition theory has found favor, especially when applied to beginners. For eager young bodybuilders, the act of getting into the gym and training is no problem – indeed, overtraining is a more likely pitfall. Hand in hand with that eagerness goes a positive mental attitude. But nutrition? Well, nutrition is very often the poor relation.

While beginners, in pursuit of drawing up training schedules, are willing to splash around more ink than found in War and Peace, very few will bother to put pen to paper and list their dietary needs. If you're really serious about your bodybuilding, keep in mind that nutrition is the tool with which you augment your work done in the gym.

Support the intensity of your workouts with an equally committed approach to nutrition and your gains will not only be greater, they will come quicker and you will feel healthier and more enthused.

Even though I rate nutrition as an essential part of the muscle-building quartet, it does not have to be a complex subject to understand. The rules of nutrition as they apply to accumulating lean body tissue are relatively simple and logical.

The following questions represent the topics that I am asked about most frequently concerning diet. The answers offer a step-by-step guide to success in an area that is too often overcomplicated by jargon and information irrelevant to beginning and intermediate bodybuilders.

What should be the first step in formulating my diet?

The starting point is to determine the amount of nutritious calories you will need in order to start increasing your bodyweight via lean muscle. We'll come to the protein/carbohydrate/fat breakdown in due course, but first let's deal with calories as a total. To gain extra muscle, you have to consume more calories than the quantity required to keep your present bodyweight stable. Each of us (due to personal factors like bodyfat/muscle composition, metabolic rate, etc.) has an individual capacity to burn calories. There's no golden rule that decrees that every 160-pound person burns X amount of calories. Thus, calorie intake and output has to be a totally individual assessment.

Obtain a book on nutrition that lists the amount of calories contained in each individual food product. Over a seven-day period, log the food you eat and then compute the total amount of calories consumed. Divide that figure by seven and – providing your bodyweight remains static – you have the daily calorie figure that maintains your bodyweight. Increase that daily allowance by 500 nutritious calories and, unless a metabolic problem exists, you should be in a bodyweight-gaining mode.

What is a reasonable rate of bodyweight increase?

You should be aiming for an increase of one to two pounds of bodyweight per month. You can build muscle only at a certain rate: If you're experiencing a gain far in excess of three pounds a month, it's likely the gain will comprise more fat than muscle.

If my bodyweight remains the same after increasing my calories, what should I do?

Let's take the example of someone who has computed his bodyweight-maintenance level as being 3,000 calories, and has therefore increased his daily caloric intake to 3,500. If, after two weeks, his bodyweight has remained static, he should boost his daily intake by a further 400 calories. Always up the ante in small increments. In all aspects of bodybuilding (training and diet), I advocate that whatever changes are made be completed gradually. A gradual approach to change makes it so much easier to monitor the effect, or lack of effect, of those changes. For instance, if you totally altered your diet in one fell swoop and radically revamped your training schedule at the same time, the transformation would be too dramatic for you to assess the factors that had actually generated change, if any.

What percentage breakdown of nutrients should I aim for?

On a daily basis, the total calories you consume should be constituted as follows: 50-55% carbohydrate, 30% protein and 15-20% fat. Again, a dietary handbook will list which foods fall into which category and the calorie count for each.

The percentage of fat advised is higher than I would recommend to an advanced bodybuilder, where the figure would be 10-15%. The reason is that a beginner is concerned with gaining bodyweight – good bodyweight – and a fat content of 15-20% is not going to hurt that purpose. Those still in their teens or early twenties will be happy to learn that their metabolisms allow them to burn fat more efficiently than trainers of more mature years.

What do each of the macronutrients do?

Protein is the main element in the construction, maintenance and repair of muscle tissue. To build extra muscle, the body must be provided with adequate amounts of protein on a regular basis. A consistent supply of protein (five or six servings a day, spaced three or so hours apart) keeps the body in a state of positive nitrogen balance: the condition that facilitates muscle growth. I would recommend that a bodybuilder maintain a daily intake of 1 1/4 grams of protein per pound of bodyweight.

Carbohydrate provides a bodybuilder with his main energy source. Without an adequate intake of carbohydrates, you are not providing the body with the fuel necessary to power your workouts. In a deficient carbohydrate state, the body will recruit its protein stores as an alternative source of energy. The protein will be broken down into amino acid form, and then further refined into glucose, which will be used as energy. You'll be burning muscle for energy. A diet insufficient in carbohydrate therefore leads to your protein intake not being put to optimum use for muscle building and repair.

Fat acts as a secondary energy source (particularly when aerobic activity is undertaken), as well as fulfilling an important role in the absorption of various vitamins. It also helps to lubricate joints, cushion internal organs and keep skin tissue healthy. Fat also aids in maintaining the efficiency of the nervous system and is involved in the production of the body's natural hormones. Some bodybuilders are fanatical about keeping their fat intake as low as possible, but you can't function without it. I never drop below an intake of 10%.

Which foods are best for bodybuilding purposes?

Protein sources should be drawn from eggs (mixed in the ratio of one yolk to four egg whites), chicken, turkey, fish and lean red meat. Low-fat milk is another form of first-class protein, but a lot of people don't digest it or other dairy products very well.

Carbohydrates are best sourced from oatmeal; rice; potatoes; pasta; fibrous vegetables like broccoli, cauliflower or salads; and fruits like apples, bananas and oranges.

Fats should be consumed as a byproduct of your protein intake, as well as from the vegetable fat found in many carbohydrate products.

How many meals should I eat each day?

Muscle growth is better stimulated if the body is continually topped up with the appropriate nutrients. That means abandoning the traditional three-meal-a-day timetable (breakfast, lunch, dinner) and converting to a program in which you eat six or seven meals a day, separated by intervals of three hours or so. Only so many nutrients can be absorbed at any one sitting, so this more frequent eating plan ensures that you are continually supplying your body with muscle-building ingredients. As stated previously (but it is worth reiterating), this approach will keep the body in a positive state of nitrogen balance: the condition in which muscular growth is stimulated.

The accompanying dietary chart (Table One) represents a typical day's eating plan for someone consuming 3,500 calories.

What basic supplementation program would you suggest?

For those who are really serious about maximizing bodybuilding gains, here's a list of the supplements I strongly advise you to include in your dietary program.

Protein powders

A quality protein supplement is a convenient and cost-effective way to ensure that you are consuming sufficient amounts of protein throughout the day. Many people find it difficult and inconvenient to take in 200-300 grams of protein per day from solid foods. The most efficient protein powder on the market at the moment would appear to be ion-exchange whey protein, which has a higher biological-value rating than eggs, previously considered to be the best source of protein.

Multivitamin/mineral pack

As a bodybuilder, you are putting an increased – and unusual – amount of stress on your body. This means your intake of vitamins and minerals should be above the RDA (Recommended Daily Allowance). The RDA for vitamins and minerals is to ensure against deficiencies for the normal sedentary person, not to support optimum athletic performance. In my opinion, you will need far in excess of the RDA amounts. I recommend a multivitamin/mineral supplement containing at least 1,000 milligrams (mg) of vitamin C, 50 mg of B-complex and 400 IU of vitamin E.

Extra minerals

Minerals are crucial to the total well-being and healthy functioning of the body. I would recommend that, as well as the amounts contained in the multivitamin/mineral pack, you take the following three minerals in the prescribed daily doses: 1,000 mg Calcium; 500 mg Magnesium; and 50 mg Zinc.

Rewards of Good Nutrition

Vitamin C

I am a big believer in vitamin C. Vitamin C is essential to the recuperation and repair processes, and it protects against colds and infections. In addition to your multivitamin, I recommend that you take an extra 500 mg at three mealtimes spread throughout the day.

Creatine

This is a natural substance that raises levels of ATP (adenosine triphosphate), which is the fuel for muscular contractions. Athletes using creatine have consistently reported increased bodyweight, strength and power. Most manufacturers recommend a period of loading (20 grams daily), followed by a smaller maintenance amount (five grams daily). However, recent studies seem to indicate that the loading stage may not be necessary and smaller daily amounts (around five grams) may result in greater long-term benefits.

Glucosamine/Collagen Hydrolysate

Taken in combination, these two items have been shown to protect the structural integrity of joints and ligaments. With consistent long-term use, they help to repair and form new cartilage in damaged joints.

Carbohydrate-powder postworkout drink

To help maximize recovery and recuperation, I highly recommend a postworkout drink formed from a carbohydrate powder. This powder should consist primarily of simple carbs, i.e., sucrose or dextrose. Ingesting these simple sugars will cause an insulin release. Insulin is a storage hormone, and its release will push glucose and amino acids toward the stressed muscle tissue, which will aid in the recuperation and repair processes. After a workout is the only time I feel simple sugars should be consumed. The rest of the day, you should concentrate on complex carbohydrates that don't cause such a rapid insulin release. As an example, a postworkout drink for a 200-pound bodybuilder should contain 70 grams of carbs and 30 grams of whey protein. This drink should be taken immediately after a workout and followed by a balanced meal within one to one and a half hours later.

What are the biggest dietary mistakes?

A lot of bodybuilders, especially beginners, go on a crazy bulking-up program in which they eat everything that doesn't move. They rack up huge calories and huge fat deposits. You can't force-feed your way to muscle gains. Unless you're a physiological freak, you can stimulate no more than a couple of pounds of muscle growth a month. Any weight gain in dramatic excess of that will be mostly in the form of fat. Once excess fat is deposited and lingers awhile, it becomes difficult to shed.

At the other extreme are those who underestimate diet. Their shortcomings include not eating enough; eating irregularly; and focusing purely on calories eaten and not the protein/carbohydrate/fat breakdown of those calories. In short, they follow a diet with no set muscle-building parameters.

If there is one secret to bodybuilding, it is consistency: consistency of training; consistency of dietary input; consistency of mental application. Follow the dietary guidelines outlined here and – harnessed with the other two components – consistency of progress will be yours!

Table One

THE MUSCLE-BUILDING DIET

This eating-plan example comprises 3,500 calories broken down into a ratio of 50-55% carbohydrate, 30% protein and 15-20% fat.

7 AM
Meal one: Breakfast
100 grams oatmeal
6 egg whites
2 egg yolks
2 slices whole-wheat toast
1 banana

10 AM
Meal two: Midmorning
40 grams protein powder (mixed with water)

300 grams baked potato

1 PM

Meal three: Lunch

200 grams chicken breast

100 grams rice

100 grams mixed vegetables

4 PM

Meal four: Preworkout

40 grams protein powder (mixed with water)

1 banana

(Workout: 5 pm to 6 pm)

6 PM

Meal five: Postworkout

70 grams carbohydrate powder

30 grams protein powder

7 PM

Meal six: Evening dinner

200 grams extra-lean beef

300 grams baked potato

200 grams broccoli

10 PM

Meal seven: Supper

40 grams protein powder

50 grams oatmeal

* This meal plan is based on a 5 PM workout. If you train at a different time, revamp this schedule so that the preworkout and postworkout meals bookend your training.

TEN TIPS TO EATING SUCCESS

1) Obtain a nutrition book that lists the calorie amount and protein/carbohydrate/fat breakdown of all food products.
2) Follow a diet that consists of 50-55% carbohydrate, 30% protein and 15-20% fat.
3) Eat six or seven nutritious meals a day, spaced three hours or so apart.
4) On a daily basis, consume 1 1/4 grams of protein per pound of bodyweight.
5) Use protein shakes as an efficient means of boosting calorie intake.
6) Include a multivitamin/mineral pack as insurance against dietary deficiency.
7) Be satisfied with a bodyweight gain of one to three pounds a month.
8) Keep a formal written record of your diet so that you can accurately make and assess changes when required.
9) Institute changes gradually. Do not allow dramatic swings.
10) Be as consistent with your diet as you are with your training schedule.

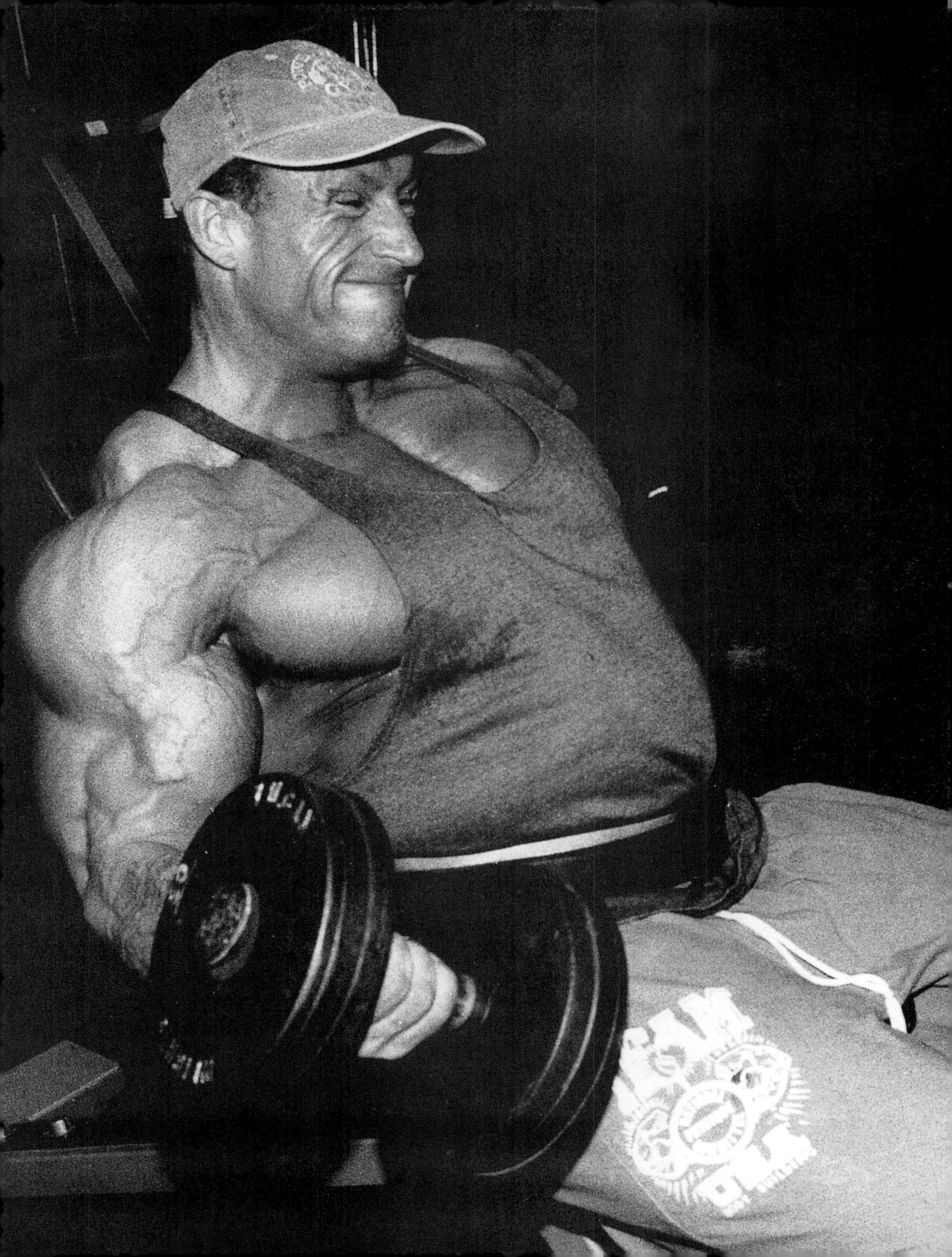

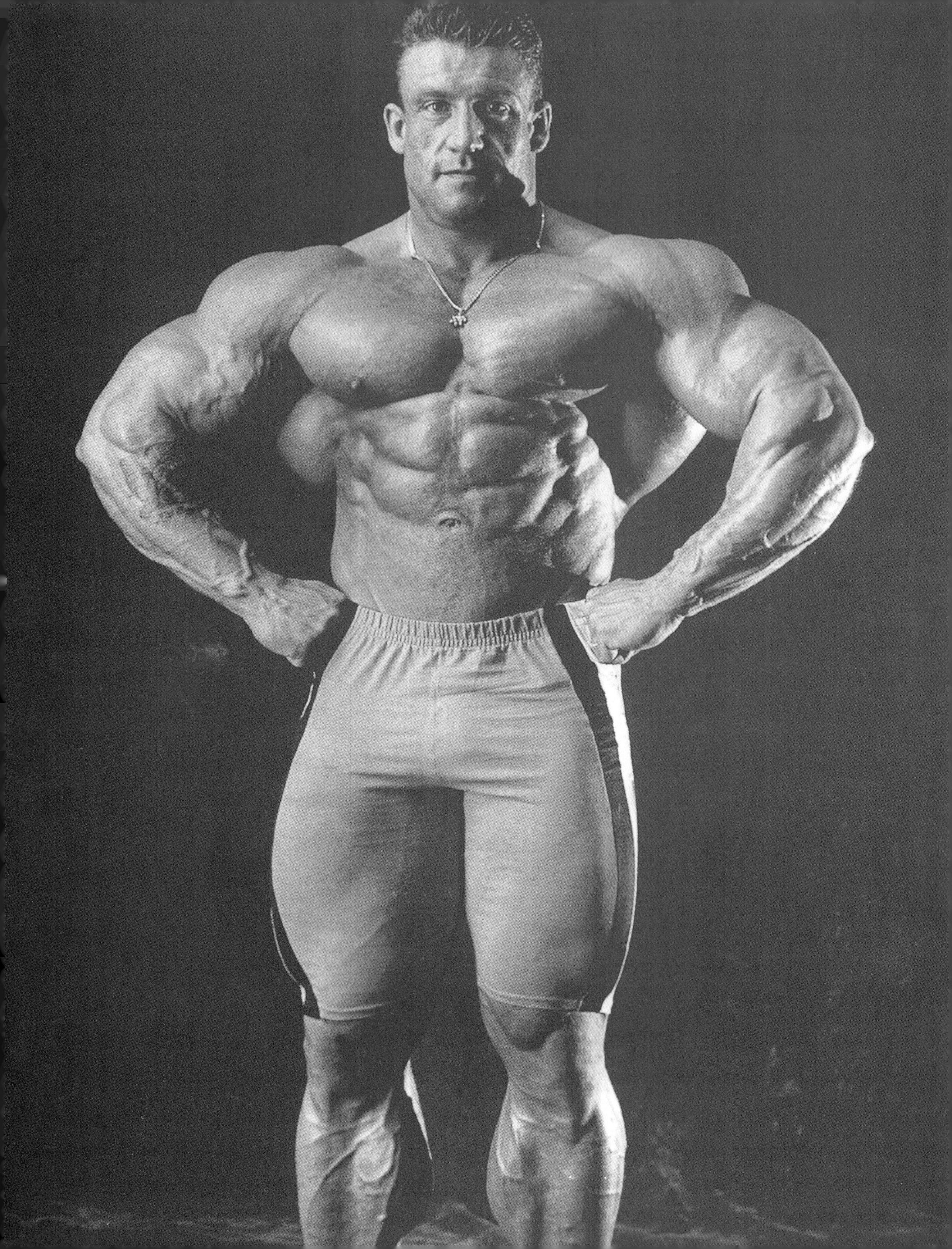

CHAPTER 18

MUSCLE INK:
The Need To Keep A Diary

Throughout this book, I have stressed the need to draw up a personalized game plan — one that suits your needs, genetics and disposition to certain exercises and training frequencies. I have also underlined the importance of analyzing and monitoring your progress, and the need to constantly fine-tune your approach based on what works for you. The simple truth is that you cannot accomplish your goals without keeping a bodybuilding diary.

Only by using a bodybuilding diary can you honestly and accurately monitor your progress, isolate problem areas and arrive at a solution. With a diary, you can be confident in the knowledge that you're acting on data that have been compiled in an "as it happened" form, and is staring back at you in unimpeachable black and white. The alternative is to rely on the vagaries of your memory and hope for the best — hardly a scientific approach. Believe me, once you start your own diary, it will quickly become a priceless asset and a constant point of reference. All the changes I've made to my training and diet over the years have been actualized only after a critical analysis of my bodybuilding diary.

Here's what you should include in yours.

WORKOUTS

You should list each and every workout in your diary. The data should include date, time and duration of your training session. You should list the exercises, the number of sets, poundages and

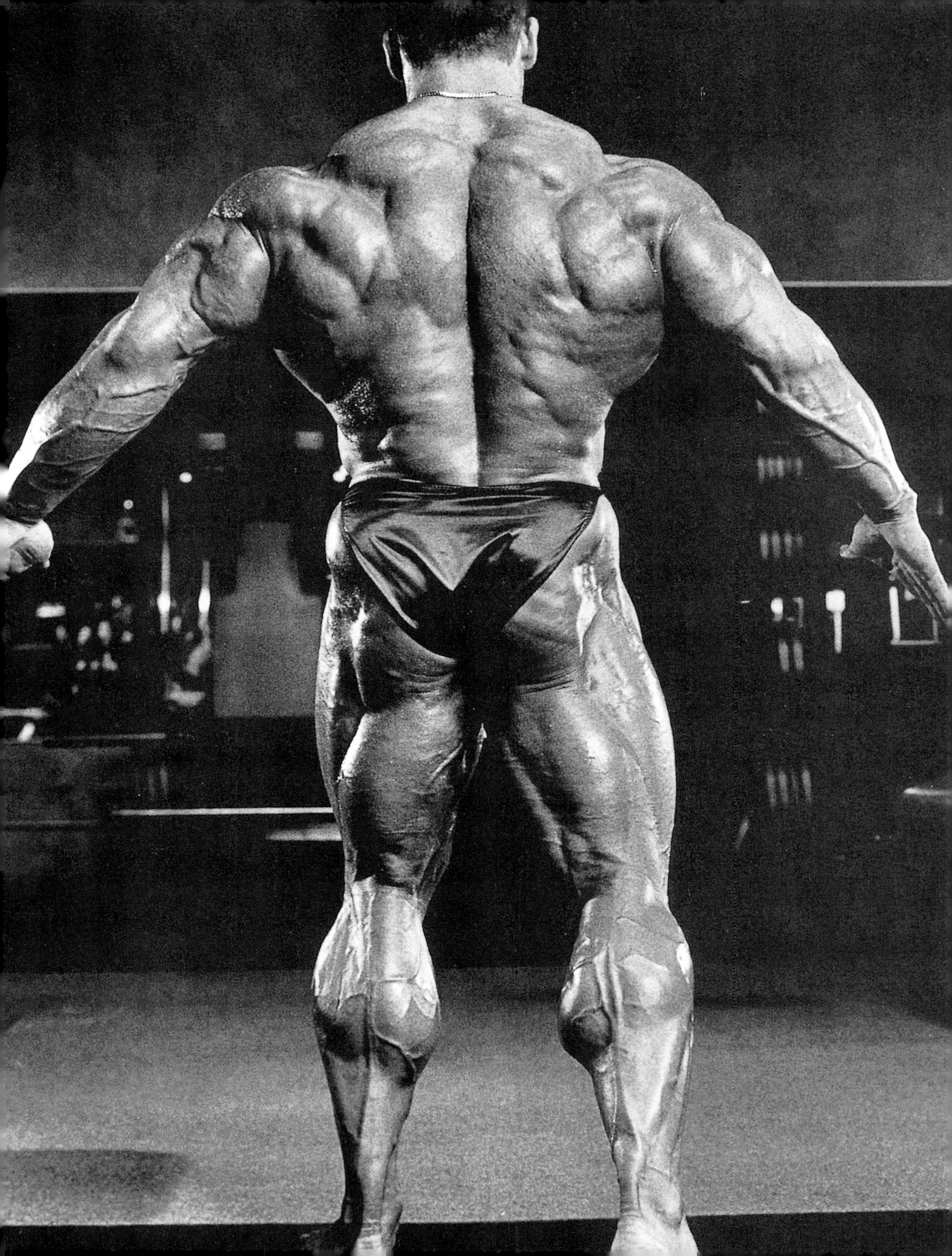

number of reps completed, including forced reps, etc. Obviously, this means you must enter information as the workout progresses.

You should also include other pertinent facts, such as new personal bests in reps completed or weight lifted. Afterward, you can examine your preceding workouts and pinpoint how you arrived at this new high. Did you train at a slower pace and have more energy reserves going into the set in question? Was it the first workout after a two-day layoff? Did you recently change the sequence of exercises? Did you concentrate more than usual on technique? The answers should be in your diary. Find the solution and then apply it to other exercises.

In the same spirit, you should underscore low points, such as a lousy workout or an injury, no matter how minor. Again, referring to past entries will help you discover why such lapses took place. Did the lousy workout come on the heels of training four times a week instead of the prescribed three? Were you out partying the previous night? Did the injury occur after you bypassed a full warm-up or attempted an extra set? Again, your diary will tell you.

A diary is also indispensable in solving the common problem of a lagging bodypart. If your biceps aren't progressing, for instance, refer to your diary. Let's say your diary tells you that you've been training biceps following a full back session. The answer would seem to be that your biceps have not recovered from all the pulling movements involved in back workouts. One solution would be to reorganize your training, so that your biceps routine does not follow back. Or you may decide to kick in an extra rest day. To fully bring biceps up to par, you should further prioritize them by training them first in your session.

Another common training problem is that of static bodyweight. Using your diary, you may discover a pattern in which your workouts have become increasingly shorter. Taking your static bodyweight into consideration, this could mean your workout pace is too fast and you're overtraining, which disturbs the recuperation cycle and limits muscular growth. The answer is to take a week off from training and return to the gym fully recuperated with a modified workout pace. Alternatively, your diary may show that your workouts have become easier and longer. This is a wake-up call telling you to accelerate the pace of your workouts and increase your poundages to hit failure honestly around the required rep range.

A diary is fundamental for monitoring, planning and fine-tuning your progress. A diary allows you to be more realistic about setting goals, both short- and long-term. If you have gained 10 pounds of quality muscle after six months of training, it would be unrealistic to expect to add another 10 pounds the following month. Your diary allows you to get to know "you" better.

DIET

You should be following a bodybuilding-oriented, highly nutritious diet as outlined in Chapter 17. Just as you do with training, you should record everything you eat on a daily basis, listing it in a meal-by-meal style. You need to log the foods eaten, the total calories, and the carb/protein/fat breakdown. I find dietary entries are best done at the end of each day.

What is also critical is to log any aberrations from the norm, such as weekend binges, or meals skipped due to illness, overtime work or any other reason. By listing these departures from your regular plan, you will be better able to gauge the impact of your nutritional habits on your workouts. Did a lousy workout follow a weekend binge? Did you lose weight after traveling and, therefore, were unable to keep your calorie count up? The answers to such dietary questions will be found in your diary.

BODYWEIGHT

You should also keep track of your bodyweight and enter it in the diary on a weekly basis. Check your bodyweight once a week on the same scales at the same time on the same day. To better standardize this information, weigh yourself first thing in the morning before you eat and after you've used the bathroom. This gives a more accurate measure of actual changes in bodyweight.

A realistic bodyweight gain is one or two pounds of quality muscle per month. By recording your bodyweight in a consistent manner, you will have an accurate reading of whether or not you're hitting that target. If you aren't, then you should increase your daily calorie count by 400 calories. If you are gaining more than that, but the gain is more fat than muscle tissue, you should reduce your calories accordingly.

Although I highly recommend that you check your bodyweight on a weekly basis, I do not advise that you measure your waist, biceps, chest, etc., with the same regularity. To do so may make you impatient for instant results. However, despite what most bodybuilders say, it is good to know your measurements. I suggest you take them every six weeks.

EXTRACURRICULAR

You should also log other activities that may have an indirect effect on your workouts. If you've worked overtime a lot, taken a vacation, moved or ended a relationship, record these things. Make a note of any occurrence that causes you to stray from your normal training habits. For example, you may find that an unscheduled weekend morning workout was more productive than your regular mid-week evening session.

Over the long haul, look for a pattern to emerge. By giving prominence to breakthroughs and plateaus, such patterns are easier to discern. Keeping a written record of them helps you form a complete picture of your performance.

CLOSING THE BOOK

Your bodybuilding diary can be kept in a proper diary as sold at a stationary or office supply store. I prefer a big, thick notebook, in which I allocate a page for each day.

Think of your training diary as being like a ship's log. Just as a ship's log charts every aspect of a particular voyage, your training diary is a record of where you've been, as well as an indicator of where you're headed and how best to get there. The longer your journey, the more useful the diary becomes. After just a few weeks, you'll realize how useful a diary can be. Just think how much more useful a library of diaries charting several years of endeavor can be. Keep at it, and you'll have such a library.

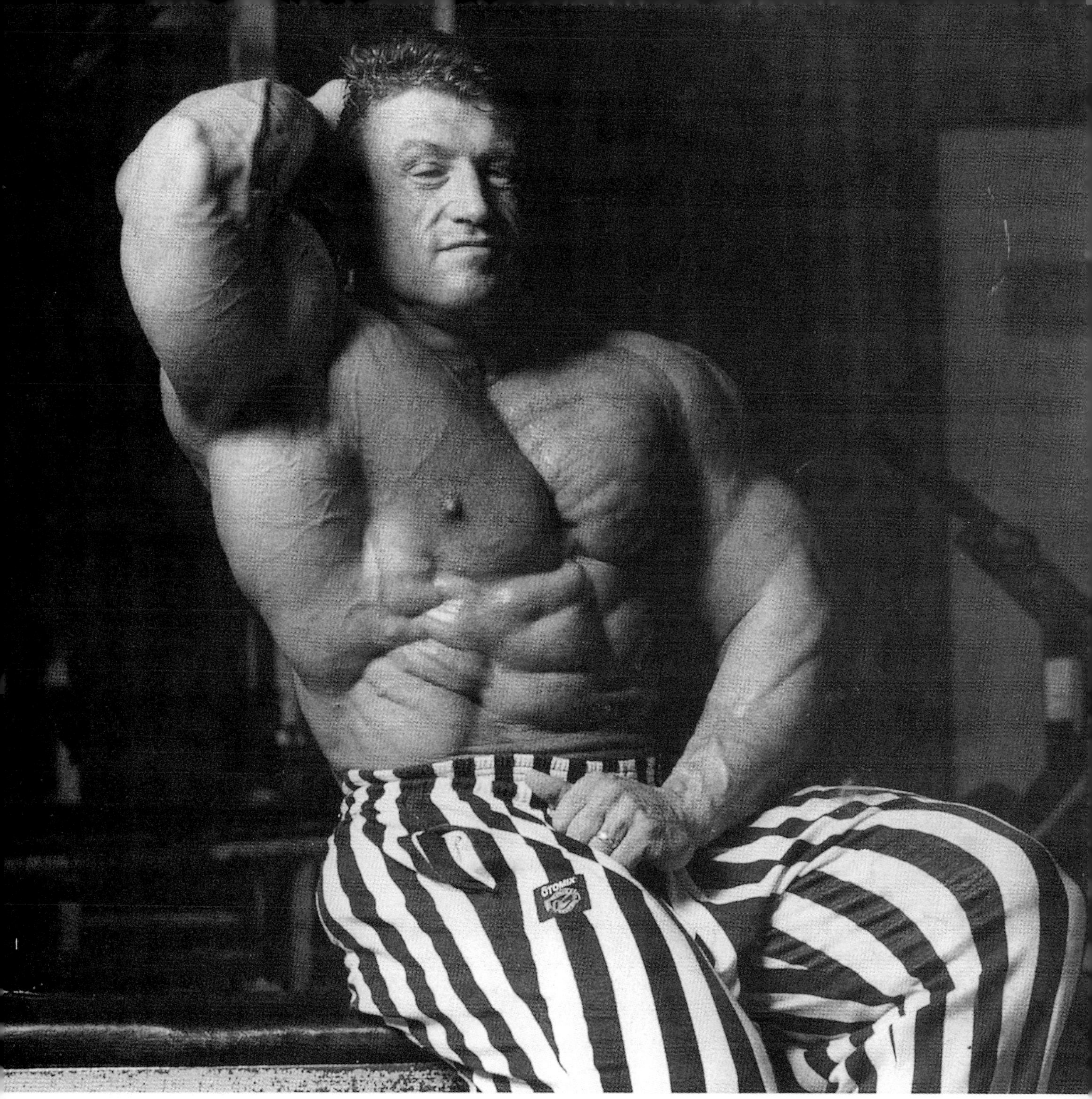
OTOMIX

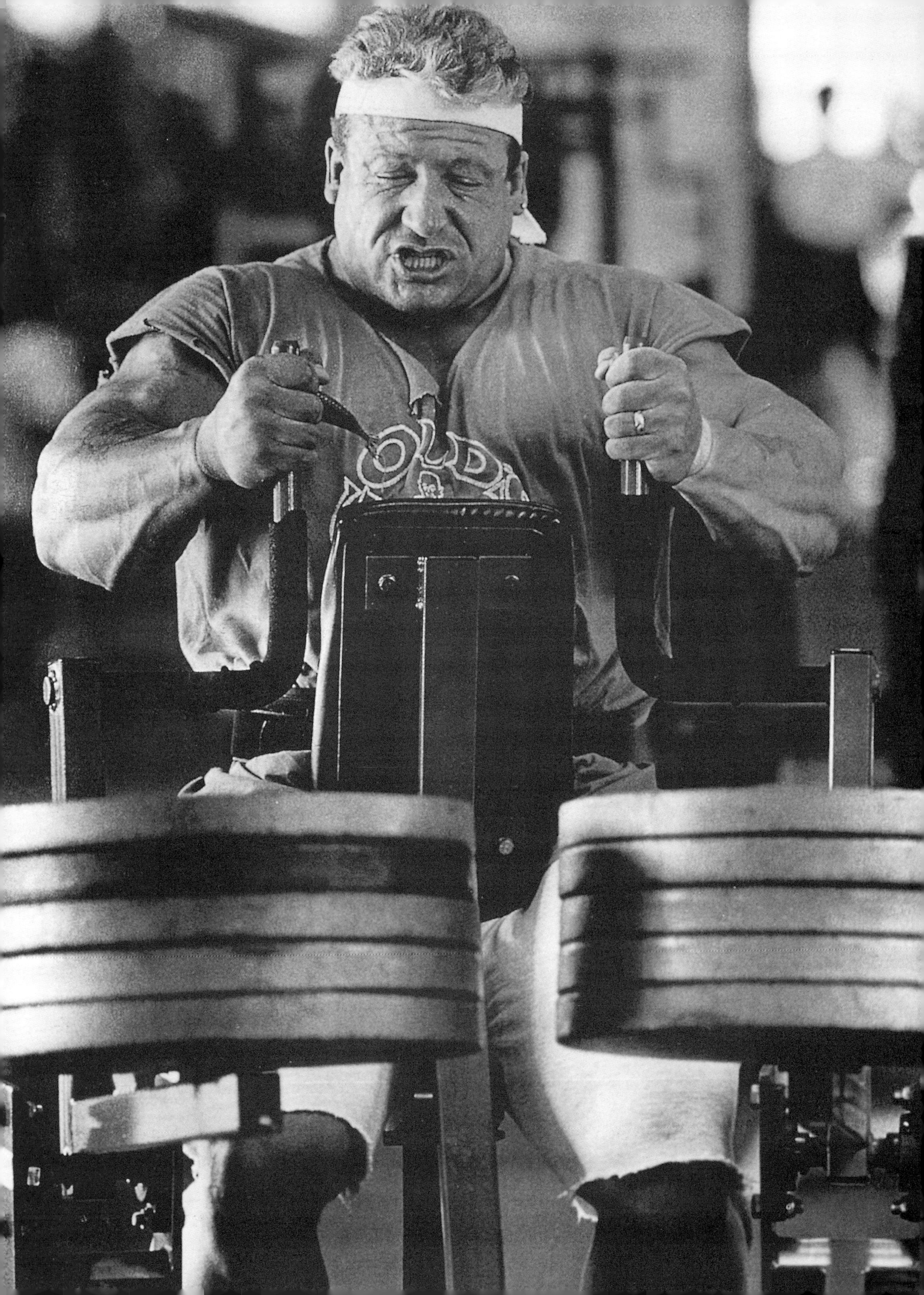

CHAPTER 19

DEVELOPING AN IRON WILL

The harshest critic of Dorian Yates' physique is me! I don't kid myself: There are many guys in the pro ranks who have better genetics than I do, so I know that the commodity that has allowed me to defeat them in Mr. Olympia competition has been my mental application and intensity. To beat guys with better genetics, I've had to be more driven, determined and disciplined than they are, otherwise I would have lost out to their superior physical inheritance.

The mental approach you adopt toward your bodybuilding career is the only constant factor of your chosen lifestyle. You don't eat or train every waking minute, but you are, or should be, mentally operational between rising and retiring. Furthermore, it is the mental process that dictates what you eat and how you train.

That's why I've always believed – and stressed – that although good genetics, correct nutrition and a scientifically thought-out training program are the fundamental building blocks for success, mental intensity is the cement that binds the whole structure together.

That marriage of physical and mental power is at its most evident and potent when my approach to a workout is examined.

IN THE MOOD

I usually work out at about 11:30 AM. Ninety minutes prior to that, I will retreat into the office housed in my home and begin to mentally lock in on the imminent workout. My wife, Debbie, understands that I'll be withdrawing into myself; she won't bother me once this process is underway.

In preparation, I'll spend 30 minutes reviewing my training diary and any other literature relevant to the upcoming workout. If, for instance, I'm due to train legs, I'll analyze my last leg workout and get a fix on the exercises, sets, reps and poundages I'll be shooting for.

I'll ask myself things like "Do I feel strong today? Am I gonna do forced reps?" or "Am I a little tired? Should I just go for eight full reps and forget forced reps?" I'll visualize myself doing the exercises. I see the plates on the bar and imagine how heavy the weight's going to feel. I see the bar bend, and I'll envisage how hard I'll have to push to move it.

What I'm doing is sorting out the workout in my mind, so that, by the time I enter the gym, it's like I just have to insert a prerecorded tape and rubber-stamp the workout. This preamble is to ensure that I'm 100% focused on the job at hand and won't arrive at the gym with the attitude of "OK, what shall I do today?"

During this period of meditation, I'll also assess whether I have fully recuperated from the previous workout, and I might make the decision not to train that day. Other times, I'll actually be warming up in the gym before realizing, No, today's not my day. I'm not fresh enough to give 100%.

If that's the case, I'll leave the gym without a shred of guilt. I don't look upon my training as a discipline I have to complete X amount of times a week. A workout is undertaken for the sole purpose of stimulating muscle growth, and if I'm not fully recuperated, I won't stimulate muscle growth.

Training merely ignites the first stage of that growth: The actual muscle growth takes place outside the gym. If my body's recuperative system is not able to respond to further muscle ignition, there's no point to the workout. I know that if I take that day off, I can come back the next day and have a tremendous workout. It's better to drop a workout and train three times a week and make progress than train six times a week and get nowhere.

COUNTDOWN TO A WORKOUT

Around 10:30 AM, I have a carbohydrate drink to boost my glycogen reserves before changing into my training gear. The preparation I undergo for a workout is almost ritualistic. I institute a chain of habit-forming checks and procedures that ultimately lead to a great workout. Even items of workout gear play a part. When training legs, I always wear the same "leg" pants. When chest is on the agenda, I don my "chest" hat. I always wear the same top to a delt workout. Those sartorial touches help to give further emphasis to the upcoming workout. Having my "leg" pants on makes me zone in even more on the agonies to come.

I leave the house around 10:45 for the 20-minute drive to my gym. During the ride, my focus on the workout becomes even more concentrated. By the time I reach the gym, I'm so into myself and psyched for the workout that I don't even acknowledge anyone who happens to be there. The regular members know the score: I'm not being rude or a prima donna, I'm there to do my job and am not really aware of anyone else.

I deliberately create a barrier so that those who don't know my modus operandi are dissuaded from approaching me. Newcomers may try to catch my eye, but when I enter the gym, I purposely desist from making eye contact. When I'm resting between sets, I'll keep my gaze on the ground. I'm not a fun guy to work out with.

I've watched guys who, before and during a training session, will horse around, shoot the breeze

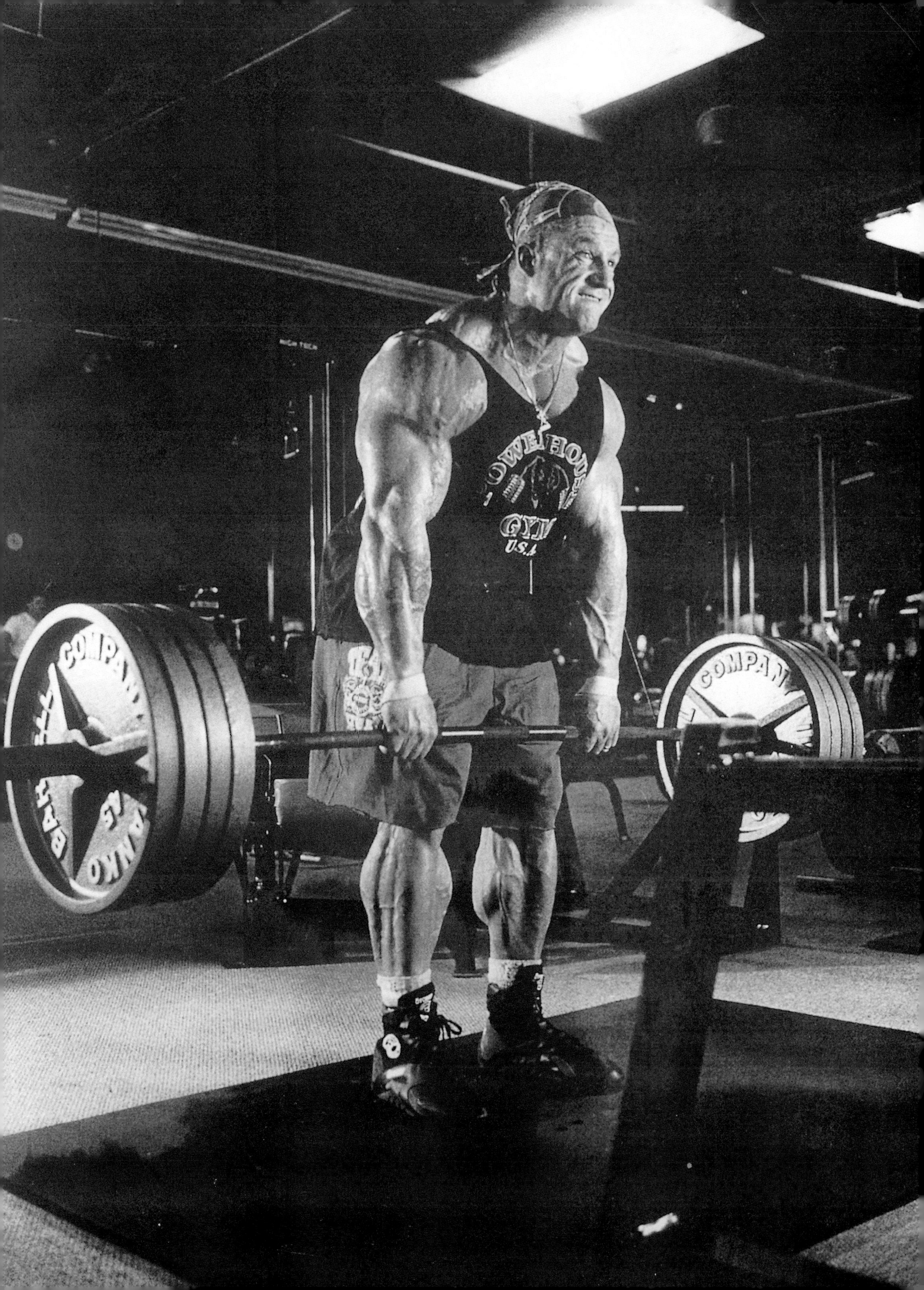
GYM
U.S.A.

and generally allow themselves to be distracted from their workouts. By retreating into myself, I'm eliminating any and all distractions, and I'm focusing totally on what I'm in the gym to do. To many, that approach may appear too intense, but as far as I'm concerned, you have to cultivate training tunnel vision. Otherwise, there's a thousand potential reasons every day to be distracted from your workout. Afterward, I'll talk and have a laugh with anyone and everyone, but, before and during a training session, my task is to channel all my aggression and energy into the workout.

I have the luxury of being able to train in my own gym at a time when there are very few people there. Taking advantage of that situation, my training partner and I, before starting a workout, will set up all the appropriate machines and bars so that everything is ready for each exercise. If we're training legs, for instance, our first job is to load the equipment for the leg extension, leg press and hack squat machine. We do this so that we're not burning up our energy hunting around the gym for plates between exercises. It's all systems go – no waiting around.

THE WORKOUT

To further reinforce a hardcore and aggressive training frame of mind, I always play a heavy-metal tape while working out. Heavy metal is raw and balls-to-the-wall stuff – just the right mood for a workout. If I train in another gym and there's a Michael Bolton tape playing, I get slightly pissed off.

Guns N' Roses is the tape I reserve for leg day only. It's another ritual: When Guns N' Roses blares out, you better know it's thigh screaming day. For other bodyparts, I usually play tapes by Aerosmith, Pearl Jam or Nirvana.

During a workout I communicate only with short sentences or a nod. Words are restricted to phrases like "Put another 20 on" or "Give me two forced reps when I ask." The last thing I want to do during a workout is discuss last night's TV shows or my partner's love life.

I've often been asked what happens if I suddenly run out of steam or hit a mental block part of the way through a workout. The truth is it never happens. My buildup to a workout is so meticulous, programmed and all-encompassing that I know before I begin that the goals I have set for that session will be achieved.

If I have the slightest inkling that I'm in for a crappy workout, the whole session is aborted by the warm-up stage at the latest. Once I give myself the green light that the workout is on, I'm fully committed to finishing it and meeting the preset demands I've scheduled for myself. There is no other option!

THE WINNING EDGE

When I compete, I walk onstage with the mindset that I am the winner. This is because I'm convinced, rightly or wrongly, that I've given more than anyone in the preparation to be there. In all aspects of my prep, I know I haven't given less than 100%, so I don't stand in a lineup thinking, Damn, I wish I hadn't taken it easy through that last workout. I shouldn't have had that cream cake. I should've done this; I should've done that.

The mental edge is the component that separates a winning competitor from a good one. I know that the main factor in my winning six Mr. Olympia titles has been my mental approach.

Think about it. Mental approach is really a cerebral interpretation of your external goals. If your goal is to win a national title, then you have to adopt the correct mental approach that will fire you toward that goal. That means sitting down and honestly asking yourself if you are genetically fit to reach that level, and whether you are willing to put in the hard work necessary in order to realize that potential. If the answer is an honest "Yes!" you have the go-ahead to draw up the appropriate game plan and pursue your goal. If you lack the mental strength – i.e., the drive, the determination and the discipline – to go forward, then all the genetics in the world won't allow you to freewheel your way to champion status.

Here is the seeming contradiction in bodybuilding: In a sport where physical prowess appears to be the most visible overriding asset, inner mental strength is the determining factor for success. The major reason I've won six Mr. Olympia titles is because I was prepared to ask more of myself mentally than other more physically gifted guys. It's called the will to win!

TEN TIPS TO GAINING A MENTAL EDGE

1) If you hit a training rut that lasts more than a week, take off a complete week from the gym.
2) During that week off, analyze your program and change it.
3) Change could mean change of exercises; change of bodypart sequence; change of sets and reps; change of training frequency; change of training environment; change of training partner; etc. Whatever is obstructing your progress, isolate and change it.
4) Always set realistic honest goals, both short-term and long-term.
5) Take time to assess your goals for a particular workout before the actual session.
6) Develop habits that tie together to form an overall plan for executing a successful workout.
7) If you are feeling overfatigued, don't be a hero: Take the day off.
8) Once committed to a workout, insist that you meet your preset goals.
9) Don't be distracted from your workout because you feel the need to be polite.
10) A stronger will can overcome superior genetics.

Dorian with the Master Blaster - Joe Weider

142   A PORTRAIT OF DORIAN YATES

CHAPTER 20

AT THE END OF THE DAY

On Sunday, September 13, 1998, I flew alone to Los Angeles. I was to meet with Joe Weider the following day to tell him that I was retiring from competitive bodybuilding. Joe, as always, was graciousness itself. He wished me well and told me I had nothing more to prove to anybody. I'm happy to report that in the entire six years of my business relationship with Joe, he and I have never had a problem. All of us in the sport owe a giant debt to the father of bodybuilding, who created the industry we enjoy.

I flew back to England the next day. I had a lot of time to think during the 12-hour flight. It hadn't sunk in yet that my search to discover how "different" I was — the journey to see how far I could take my physique — was, after 15 years of blood, sweat and tears, truly over. The realization that I would never again compete as a bodybuilder forced me to reflect on how much the sport of bodybuilding had shaped, enriched and changed my life. Most of us live from day to day, and move from one stage to another without bells and whistles signaling change is taking place. Only during periods of retrospection are we able to assess how far we've traveled. On that flight, I had such an intense moment of reflection that the entire odyssey, from my origins to my current position in life, made me feel like I was the lead character in a rags-to-riches novel.

LIFESTYLE

The most visible changes are in the lifestyle I lead today compared to my life back in 1983. The financial success of my six Mr. Olympia titles, my contracts with Joe Weider, and other business interests from bodybuilding have enabled Debbie and I to give Lewis, our 14-year-old son, the security that we as kids could only dream about. Instead of the two-bedroom council flat we shared in a rough part of Birmingham, my family and I now live in a spacious house, standing in an acre of land, in Birmingham's stockbroker belt. I mention these things not as a boast but to contrast my current life with my spare beginnings. I simply want to convince you that if you believe in yourself, as I learned to do through bodybuilding, you can achieve your goals.

Beyond the houses and cars, my bodybuilding success has also given me something even more valuable. As Mr. Olympia, I've traveled extensively, all over the United States, Canada, Europe, Australia, the Far East, you name it. This globe-trotting has afforded me an insight and education I'll carry with me the rest of my life. The enrichment of meeting all these different people has made me enjoy my life that much more.

PERSONAL

Although our material lives have changed enormously over the past decade, Debbie and I both take a quiet pride in the fact that we still spend time with the same circle of friends that we did before my success. I like to think that in basic areas of friendship, we haven't changed a bit.

I'm not going to kid anyone — I have no wish to downplay the financial benefits of my career, but just as fundamental is how the sport has shaped me as a person. Back in 1983, bodybuilding gave me a focus and a sense of purpose when I needed it most. As I look back, the realization that I fastened on to the goal of being the best bodybuilder I could be, that I set out a game plan and achieved all my objectives beyond my wildest dreams, gives me immense satisfaction.

Dorian and Debbie with friends Steve and Bev

As the plane flew through the skies that night, I thought of what my life would have been had I not found success in bodybuilding. It's not the first time I played "what if?" in thinking of my life. What would I have done if I would have been forced to earn a living outside of bodybuilding? I know some people think that I would have probably gone back to my self-destructive ways and ended up in prison or even worse. Well, I hate to spoil a good storyline, but I know I would have still have been successful in some other career. I would have been a recreational bodybuilder and taken the philosophy my sport taught me – the philosophy of realistic goal-setting and dedicating maximum effort to reach those goals – and applied it to another career. I can't guess at what I would be doing today, but I do know that I would still be thankful for being a bodybuilder.

THE OTHER DORIAN

If somebody had told me back in 1983 that, 15 years later, I would be flying first-class out of Los Angeles after visiting Joe Weider to tell him I was retiring after winning six Mr. Olympia titles, and that by that time I would be accustomed to holding two-hour seminars in front of 1,000 people, I would have laughed my Marks & Spencer's socks off. At that time the thought of public speaking would have horrified me, because I'm basically quite shy by nature — which may sound strange coming from a man who's made a career out of appearing clad in nothing but a pair of posing trunks in front of thousands of people. But over the years, bodybuilding has given me the confidence to deal with people both as individuals and in crowds.

I see public speaking duties as being part of my job as Mr. Olympia, but at other times, I'm still Dorian the introvert. For instance, after every Olympia, Debbie and I invite our friends for a celebration meal in Birmingham. Debbie will always say, "Go on, get up and give a speech." But I just can't do it, because in that environment, among friends, I'm not Mr. Olympia, I'm Dorian.

ROLE MODEL

One of the most stimulating aspects of being Mr. Olympia is the feedback I get from people all over the world saying that my training beliefs and life experiences have made a positive influence on their lives. And I get that reaction not just from bodybuilders but from people outside the sport. To think that I'm actually inspiring others to be their best is very humbling.

I receive letters from people who've lost a husband or a wife, saying my attitude of persevering against all odds helped them cope with their loss. Probably the most poignant incident was when a lady from the States came to my gym in England and told me about her son. She said that he was a great Dorian Yates fan, and had my pictures all over his room. Then he got involved in a bad car accident and was in a coma for weeks. Because he was such a great fan, his family began to regularly play my videotape, Blood & Guts, in his hospital room. Then one day while the video was playing, the stricken boy suddenly woke up, and the first thing he said was, "Is Dorian in the room? Where's Dorian?" His mother made the trip to Birmingham specifically to thank me for the effect I had had on her son. Believe me, when you hear stories like that, it makes projects like putting an extra inch on your biceps seem unimportant.

Bodybuilding truly changed my life for the better, and if my life impacts on anyone else's in a positive way, then I feel doubly blessed.

A MESSAGE FOR THE FANS

I also feel blessed by the endorsement of those who have played a part in giving me this great career. I have many people to thank, but the faction at the top of the list is the fans. For them I feel a special empathy, and my admiration and appreciation toward them is total. Indeed, the abiding memory of my competitive career is the warmth shown toward me by the fans. I've taken my lumps from some sections of the bodybuilding community, but the fans have never wavered in their support, and their faith in me has always served as a great source of inspiration. To each and everyone, I thank you for the great career your encouragement has enabled me to enjoy. Be assured, you'll still see me around the bodybuilding scene, and I'll still be in regular contact with you all through the pages of Flex and Muscle & Fitness.

Having finally called it a competitive day, do I have any regrets? How could I dare complain? I've had a fabulous career, and I leave the sport with no feelings of goals unfulfilled and absolutely no regrets. Of course, I wish I had not suffered the injuries I have, but coping with those adversities made me dig in deep and taught me a lot about myself and my capabilities. Nevertheless, I still believe fate has been on my side. Okay, I've worked very hard for my accomplishments, but there's been plenty of good fortune along the way. Mostly, I'm talking about having the good fortune of meeting Debbie and her agreeing to marry me. Without her I wouldn't be who I am today.

IT'S UP TO YOU

As you reach the end of this book, you may ask: "How does the information laid out here apply to me?" I have the privilege of talking to you as Mr. Olympia, the best in my chosen trade. But I'm not trying to tell you that by following my example, you, too, will be Mr. Olympia. My advice to anyone in any walk of life is simple: Don't start out with the thought that you're going to be Mr. Olympia, CEO of Coca-Cola, or a Nobel prize winner. Instead, just focus on a goal which constitutes the next small step of improvement. Learn to use discipline and determination to fulfill that goal. Once that goal has been reached, set the next short-term objective, and don't allow obstacles to defeat you.

In essence, whatever course you embark upon, do everything in your power to be the best that you can be. You may be surprised, like I have been, where that path may lead. Good luck to you all.

Stop Press

Dorian Yates will be developing and releasing a range of top quality Nutritional products in conjunction with Kerry Kayes and Chemical Nutritional Products.
For information and details:
Tel: (44) 161 320 8145 Fax: (44) 161 320 1212
In the UK dial: 0161 320 8145 Fax: 0161 320 1212

End of an Era